POWER DIRECT MARKETING

SECOND EDITION

POWER
DIRECT
MARKETING

SECOND EDITION

How to Make It Work for You

RAY JUTKINS

NTC Business Books
NTC/Contemporary Publishing Group

Library of Congress Cataloging-in-Publication Data

Jutkins, Ray, 1936–
    Power direct marketing : how to make it work for you / Ray
Jutkins. —2nd ed.
        p.   cm.
    Includes index.
    ISBN 0-8442-4298-5
    1. Direct marketing. I. Title.
HF5415.126.J874   1999
658.8′4—dc21   98-54274
                                                    CIP

Rev.

Interior design by Impressions Book and Journal Services, Inc.

Published by NTC Business Books
A division of NTC/Contemporary Publishing Group, Inc.
4255 West Touhy Avenue, Lincolnwood (Chicago), Illinois 60712-1975 U.S.A.
Copyright © 2000, 1994 by Ray Jutkins
Printed in the United States of America
International Standard Book Number: 0-8442-4298-5
  99 00 01 02 03 04 LB 19 18 17 16 15 14 13 12 11 10 9 8 7 6 5 4 3 2 1

CONTENTS

FOREWORD

Back in the early 1970s, I spent a summer working for my dad. Bob Hemmings, his partner, introduced me to a balding, tall, fat man with more energy than I could deal with. "Follow this guy around this summer and learn what it means to sell," Bob said. "You won't amount to anything if you can't sell like this guy!"

So, I spent 3 months in a Toyota with no air conditioning with Ray Jutkins. It was the best class I ever took. Not only wasn't there a final, but every day we made 3 to 5 calls. We had lunch with a different prospect or client—listening, learning, eating, and selling. It was the baptism of a lifetime. An over-the-top dip into the world of selling and direct response.

Three years later, having graduated with an MBA, I was back in the Toyota with Ray—listening, learning, eating, and selling. We worked together on clients like Foodmaker, Der Weinerschnitzel, Toyota, and Air New Zealand. We called on every bank, fast-food operation, savings and loan, airline, and auto manufacturer for miles. I memorized every story, every experience, and every sales technique. I learned how to make 100 phone calls a day to get 1 appointment, then make the appointment and sell the prospect.

I'm painting Ray as an energetic, persistent, driven salesman who could have sold direct marketing or swampland in Florida. Direct marketing won out. From those early days, Ray has continued his persistent form of driving enthusiasm. His excitement about offers, markets, letters, copy, art, production, and analysis is legend.

I recently spent 2 days at his home in Roll, Arizona, a forgotten and forgettable corner of Arizona where Ray finds solace and the space to create. Even in the middle of the desert, Ray finds excitement in his craft. He is constantly interrupted by clients calling from all over the world seeking his counsel. Then he makes calls to vendors demanding excellence for those same clients. Both conversations are filled with wisdom and experience.

Ray knows this business. He understands the simple beauty of response marketing and knows how to make it work. Even better, he knows how to teach the principles to people around the world who want only a response, an acceptable cost per lead, a new sale, or to reactivate a lapsed customer.

In *Power Direct Marketing*, Ray takes you on a kinetic ride through the basics of this direct marketing art form. He tells you the secrets, reveals the best ideas, and gives you the tools that will make you successful. You may use this as a handbook or just a launching pad to professionalism. You may find it elementary or advanced. No matter. If you find the book at all, you will benefit from its wisdom.

The biggest problem in direct marketing today is the tendency of many up-and-coming stars among us to think they know everything. This book will let them know they are wrong. There is a lot to learn, a lot to practice, and lots of keys to their future success.

This book will be a treasure for your library. It is jammed full of simple facts, ideas, and principles many marketers have forgotten. It will help you become a professional in this wonderful world of direct marketing. I even believe there is an idea in here that will make you a lot of money.

Read it. Enjoy it. And above all, practice it.

E. Jeffery Smith
Chairman
Smith Harrison Direct
Salt Lake City, Utah

Chapter 1

IN THE BEGINNING

HOW TO BE AN OVERNIGHT SENSATION WITH POWER DIRECT MARKETING

■ ■ ■

Now that we are in the 21st century, it may be important to consider how power direct marketing, as an idea, began.

It started in the middle of the 20th century—1960—although, of course, I didn't know it then. I was working in the passenger department of Matson Lines, a major Pacific steamship company. I worked first with travel agents and second with prospective passengers who wanted to take luxury cruises to Hawaii and the South Pacific.

Steamship carriers then, as today, ran glorious, full-page color advertisements in travel magazines and selected placements in newspaper travel sections across America. Most of the ads had coupons with the address of Matson Lines' headquarters in San Francisco. There was no telephone number to call (the 800, 888, and other toll-free numbers had not been created yet). Every day, the mailman (yes, it was a mail*man* in those days) would bring a batch of coupons from people seeking literature and schedules, prices and information for various island destinations. I would make certain the appropriate fulfillment package was prepared and shipped by return mail.

Each coupon had a line that read: "My travel agent is _____." If that line was filled in, I'd pass the lead along to the appropriate travel agent. If it was not, I got involved in the sales process. The mail was followed with an outbound telemarketing call. We didn't call it "telemarketing" or "telesales" or "tele-anything"; it was just a straight sales call. Nothing was "organized." There were no scripts, no call guides. I just picked up the phone and called. Amazingly enough, the program was outstandingly successful. It amounted to an integrated, multimedia, direct response marketing program that worked. We could measure the results.

■ WHAT DIRECT RESPONSE DOES ■

Every decade or so a new study comes out confirming, again, what we've all known all along: offering excellent service to customers is mandatory if you expect to keep them and grow your business.

Customers leave—change from one company to another—for 5 primary reasons:

1. They aren't there anymore. They move, get promoted, quit, transfer, or die. They are no longer in a position to make a buying decision. There is little you can do about this. (This reason has appeared in every study I've ever seen.)
2. They change to another supplier because a friend or business associate suggested they do so. We call this the "brother-in-law syndrome." Stay in touch with these folks. Many times, they will return to you—often, quickly.
3. They change to the competition because they have a true, competitive advantage—a major price difference or other honest benefit offered—over your product or

service. You can sell against this, yet only for so long. You have to either improve your offering or realize this is lost business.

4. They change because they are unhappy with the results of the service or product you provide. Sometimes it is personal, a people thing. Sometimes it is "general dissatisfaction" and they want to try something new.

5. They change because of a lack of caring expressed by some person(s) inside your company. Little or no contact; indifference; missed dates; budgets off target; a lack of caring expressed by sales, service, shipping, accounting, or management personnel—anyone. This *is* a reason you can do something about!

Direct marketing has become an accepted and important part of many companies' plans. It isn't the cure to every sales and marketing ill. Yet, as a discipline, it can get your prospects and keep your customers buying from you.

There are 5 primary functions of direct response marketing:

- To get new customers
- To keep the customers you already have
- To upgrade your current customers
- To cross-sell your customer base
- To keep them all coming back for more

Let's talk about each of these points one by one.

Getting New Customers

All companies want new customers. If you don't chase new customers, you soon go out of business. Why? Look at the reasons I just quoted. Even if you don't have a customer service problem, you do or will have one or more of the other challenges. It can't be helped.

Table 1.1 ▪ Your Annual Revenue Loss

Customers Lost per Day	Amount customer spends per week				
	$5	$50	$100	$200	$300
1	$94,900	$949,000	$1,898,000	$3,796,000	$5,694,000
2	189,800	1,898,000	3,796,000	7,592,000	11,388,000
5	474,500	4,745,000	9,490,000	18,980,000	28,470,000
10	949,000	9,490,000	18,890,000	37,960,000	56,940,000
20	1,898,000	18,980,000	37,960,000	75,920,000	113,880,000
50	4,745,000	47,450,000	94,900,000	189,800,000	284,700,000
100	9,490,000	94,900,000	189,800,000	379,600,000	569,400,000

You MUST look for new business. *Teleconnect*, a telecommunications publication, produced the dramatic chart shown in Table 1.1. It illustrates what happens financially when you lose a customer, whatever the reason.

Shocking, isn't it! You MUST look for new business!

Please do not let what happened to me happen to you. It was my own fault. I was not looking for new business. Why? Because I was so "busy" handling the 3 major clients that were my responsibility. I was an account executive with a large direct mail marketing agency. And, as it is easy to do, I got busy with activities. I was doing things—probably all justifiable—working with my clients.

Then 2 major events drastically changed the situation. First, 1 of my 3 key accounts went belly-up with no warning. It literally happened overnight. One third of my business was gone instantly. Next, within 60 days, a second client walked out the door. They had made a business decision they didn't want to deal with me or the agency anymore. This also was a sudden move with no warning; it just happened one afternoon. The second third of my business disappeared instantly.

So, within 60 days I lost two thirds of my business. And because I had not been prospecting for new business, it took 9 months just to get even. It was a lesson I've never forgotten. To this day, I spend some time every week prospecting for new business. Prospecting is always on my "to do" list.

San Francisco Embroidery Works (SFEW) seeks new business each month in airline magazines by running a catalog offer in small space ads with a toll-free number. This message reaches sales and marketing professionals who order high-quality, personalized corporate wearing apparel. Sometimes SFEW uses postcard decks and small classified ads in business and advertising publications. Every month it is in the marketplace, visible, looking for new business.

Gordon & Schwenkmeyer, a telemarketing company, wanted to expand its business-to-business clientele. First, it selected a tight list by both geographic location and Standard Industrial Classification (SIC) code. Next, representatives telephoned each firm on the list to verify the name, title, and address. Then they did a 3-part direct mail lead generation program. All of this to get new business.

Charles Schwab, the discount broker, uses television, radio, newspaper, selected magazines, and the World Wide Web on a continuing basis, month after month, seeking new customers for its services. The National Swimming Foundation put together a select mailing list of prospects and sought donations from them to support the amateur swimming programs in the United States. The Pizza Man, a small local eatery in southern California, uses cooperative or marriage mail on a regular basis—each time with a value-added coupon—to gain new business.

Getting new business is one effective way you can use the techniques of direct response marketing.

Keeping the Customers You Already Have

Everyone wants to keep all their good customers. It is hard work to find and get customers—it is important to keep them.

Keeping customers sold is almost a full-time job. Direct response offers many opportunities for you to do this; after all, they *are* your customers. You know them, they know you. Your message to them will most probably be heard, read, and understood.

Those in fund-raising (Save the Children, Save the Whales, the Red Cross, the Salvation Army, and so on) and those in mail order (L. L. Bean, Lands' End, Neiman Marcus, Victoria's Secret, Viking

Products, Quill, and others) do the best job at working to keep their customers. The Company Store in La Crosse, Wisconsin, frequently sends me a catalog. I bought from them in the recent past and am a very satisfied customer. They know this because I told them. So, they chase me for more.

The Winn Corporation of Seattle, Washington, offers original art to corporations. It uses a series of catalogs, special mailings, and local art shows to constantly stay in touch with its customers.

Contact Lumber Company of Portland, Oregon, uses mail and an intensive telephone campaign to service its clients. Likewise, HydraBaths, a specialty plumbing and fixture supplier in southern California, services its nationwide customer base of 800 firms via direct mail and phone.

McMurry Publishing in Phoenix, Arizona, uses an ongoing direct mail campaign to support its sales and service team. Team members follow up with phone, fax, and e-mail, visiting customers according to a scheduled plan.

Corporate Mailing Services of Toronto, Ontario, uses mail and a seminar series to stay in touch with its customers.

Kerry Candles of Carlsbad, California, is a heavy user of direct mail, with a catalog and some print ads. It offers both inbound and outbound telemarketing as its prime outreach to customers.

The smallish Meat & Fish Fellows, an Arizona-based home-delivery service, is wonderful. It uses simple direct mail with a telephone chase to stay in close touch with all its customers. It works.

Citibank in Japan uses direct mail, newsletters, in-branch materials, the Web, and an extensive telemarketing team to reach out to its growing customer marketplace.

You can keep the customers you already have. These companies do; you can too.

Upgrading Your Current Customers

Murray Raphel calls it the "loyalty ladder" (see Figure 1.1). The ladder begins at the bottom rung with *suspects*. Suspects are those folks who, on paper, look as if they can buy what you sell. You pick your

Figure 1.1 ■ The Loyalty Ladder

suspects; they don't choose you. *Prospects* are suspects who receive your marketing message, raise their hands and say, "Sure, I'll consider what you have to offer. Talk with me."

Customers are new buyers—those who buy from you the first time, probably with a small financial commitment. They dip their toe in the water to learn whether you will satisfy their needs.

Clients are your best customers. You know the 80/20 rule, where 80% (well, maybe not 80%—yet most) of your business comes from only 20% of your customers. That 20% are clients.

Then there are *advocates*, your very best clients, at the top of the ladder. They are the ones who buy from you and only from you. They recommend you, they give you testimonials, they become case history stories for you to share. They make you successful.

All of us are advocates for certain products and services. I am an advocate for Friendly Dry Cleaners in Venice, California, as well as the nearby Siam Best, an excellent Thai restaurant. Harrah's Hotel in South Lake Tahoe, Nevada, is my favorite in the world. And Chretins, a family-owned Mexican restaurant in Yuma, Arizona, can always count on me. You may prefer a certain shopping center, mail-order house, destination resort, or even garage mechanic (if you can find a good one).

In our business, all of us want more advocates. None of us will ever have enough. How do you get your customers to become clients and then move them up to advocate status? One thing you do is upgrade. You move them up from one level to another. You offer them an opportunity to make an increased buying decision.

When you decide you need a new car you usually have some idea what you want. Maybe not exactly, yet, you've probably decided on the style, very likely the make, maybe even the model. You know what you're looking for, what options you want, and what you're willing to pay. What happens when you visit the dealership? The sales rep "upgrades" you to the next model or a fancier version of what you picked. Leather seats, more buttons to push, extra trim, a better sound system—"extras" you had NOT planned on. You've just been upgraded.

Fast-food restaurants do it with "sizing." For just a little bit more money you get more food. The bank does it with designer checks. You need a simple, basic checking account. You get upgraded to a series of checks with pictures. Are they worth more than those without? No, but they sure do look nice. And they make you feel so good.

Credit card companies are wonders at upgrading. Not long ago, Wells Fargo did it to me—again. This time, they gave me a new platinum card I hadn't asked for. At the same time, they increased my credit line. I got upgraded 2 ways without saying a word.

The telephone companies in North America are as good as it gets in upgrades. British Columbia Telephone of Vancouver uses mail, followed by an outbound telemarketing call to its business customers. They offer enhanced services (upgrade).

Companies in the "supplies" business upgrade you when you call in your regular order. Many mail-order companies offer upgrades based on the amount you spend. Some offer seasonal upgrades. For others, "automatic" upgrades are made when you reach a certain spending level.

The world's major airlines have made a science of knowing their better customers. For me, as a flyer with 100,000+ miles a year on United since the frequent flyer programs began, I experience upgrades because United chooses to treat their best customers best.

Many companies offering their services over the World Wide Web give you the opportunity to upgrade when you do business with them on-line. They want to increase Web action, and one way is to offer upgrades to those who respond via that medium.

Direct response—and particularly with the telephone, where personal interaction is instant and you can respond immediately—offers you an excellent opportunity to upgrade your customers.

Cross-Selling Your Customer Base

Your best source of new business is your current customer. The easiest people to cross-sell to another level of your business are the customers with whom you already do business. Why? Because they know you and you know them. You have already established a "working with" relationship.

The Bank Marketing Association recently shared some interesting statistics from the financial marketplace. They found the odds of keeping your customer increases dramatically with the number of services that customer uses.

The following table shows the chance of a bank customer remaining a customer, based on the products/services they purchase:

Checking account only	50%
Savings account only	66%
Checking and savings accounts	90%
Checking and savings accounts and a loan	95%
Checking and savings accounts, a loan, and a safe deposit box	99%

In those parts of the world where checking accounts are a part of life, they are available on almost every street corner. They are not hard to open or close. So, if that is a bank's total relationship with a customer, it has no better than a 50/50 chance of keeping that customer. Savings accounts are a little more of a commitment. The odds increase to 2 to 1 that the bank will keep the customer. When you combine checking with savings, the odds take another large leap up. Add a loan of any type and they increase more. Include an inexpensive safe deposit box and that customer is with you for life.

Every financial institution I've worked with knows these numbers are true. Citibank around the world uses direct mail, the telephone, and now the Web to cross-sell current customers. West Coast–based Wells Fargo Bank is a major player in the direct marketing discipline in the United States. Ditto for BankOne of Columbus, Ohio, and Bank of America of San Francisco. Many of these financial giants were "old and stodgy." Today, they have stormed into the 21st century with a series of integrated multimedia advertising and direct marketing programs, aggressively offering new products and services to their current customers.

Many other industries also use direct response to cross-sell. Open any department store or oil company bill, or something from American Express, or AT&T, and what falls out (besides the financial greeting)? A billing insert with an offer selling you something— cross-selling you another product, another service.

The last time you sailed through a fast-food drive-through window you were probably asked, "Would you like an apple turnover today?"

Visit your favorite men's or women's specialty shop, make any purchase, and a cross-sell opportunity presents itself. If the salespeople are good they'll ask you to look at the accessories, a complementary tie, a matching pair of shoes, something. They'll cross-sell.

Direct response offers many cross-selling opportunities. When you use the phone as your marketing and sales tool, it becomes an obvious benefit ("Wouldn't you like to take advantage of today's telephone special?"). Use direct response marketing to cross-sell to your current customers.

Keeping Them All Coming Back for More

You get your customers, you keep them, you cross-sell and upgrade them—then you keep them coming back for more (and more).

Airline frequent flyer promotions are designed to do just that. They offer you benefits for loyalty (the programs are misnamed; they are not about frequency, they ARE about loyalty). My seminar and consulting business takes me around the world several times each year. And I'm loyal to United Airlines and their partners. Why?

Because it is to my benefit. United stays in close touch with me through direct mail 16 to 20 times a year, e-mail, and newsletters. They offer an unlisted toll-free number for me to call for assistance, reservations, anything. They are taking care of their customer.

Only your imagination limits how you might make use of the frequency/loyalty concept. For example, an innovative parking lot owner in Dallas, Texas, has a frequent parking program.

Traffic building for retail stores is an ongoing need. Direct mail is becoming more and more evident as the answer, with special messages aimed at special customers making special offers.

Judd Goldfeder of The Customer Connection in Escondido, California, puts together frequency/loyalty direct mail programs for restaurants. The food industry traditionally advertises to get you to come in and then must do it all over again—and again. Judd's service allows the restaurants to know their customers and to make them more loyal.

Leasametric, an instrument and computer equipment leasing company in northern California, uses direct response to keep in touch with its best customers. Mail supports the sales staff, an in-depth catalog is offered to those who qualify, and the telemarketing team stays in touch.

The Heritage Capital Corporation, with offices in the United States and Europe, uses direct response to reach its audience of numismatic enthusiasts, inviting them to auctions, special conventions, and other events. Selected customers are given special mail-order–only opportunities, with a constant flow of direct mail, catalogs, and audiotape messages. I've been on the company's mailing list and can testify they keep coming at you!

Any company with an outside dealer or distribution network will find direct response tools helpful. You can stay in front of your ultimate buyer and user directly by working with your independent dealer. And, for the most part, these dealers are just that—independent. They represent you and others. You are not necessarily their first thought every morning. Direct mail, the phone and fax, e-mail, and a Web site allow you to reach more of your audience with your message. And to keep them coming back for more.

▪ 25 Ways to Use Direct Response ▪

What can you do with direct response marketing today? How can you become an overnight sensation with power direct marketing in the 21st century? There are scores—probably hundreds—of different marketing and sales tasks that can effectively and efficiently be accomplished using direct response marketing techniques. Here is a list of 25:

1. Provide sales leads (lead generation)
2. Upgrade "suspects" to "prospects" so you can turn them into first-time customers
3. Reduce the cost of selling your product or service
4. Provide important sales information to your marketplace
5. Make announcements to your best industry prospects and customers
6. Counter your stiffest competition
7. Sell directly: go into the mail-order business
8. Force distribution of your product
9. Provide super service to your customers
10. Provide marketing support to your advertising media
11. Promote memberships and renewals of services
12. Create attendance at seminars, conferences, and trade shows of all kinds
13. Generate store traffic at point of sale
14. Provide an individualized message to a target audience
15. Reduce the number of sales calls needed to gain a close
16. Sell small and marginal accounts that cannot be sold economically face-to-face
17. Introduce new products and services to the marketplace
18. Reinforce outside sales efforts and support the field sales force
19. Support the in-house (telemarketing) sales force and customer service efforts
20. Increase trade show floor traffic and results

21. Conduct market surveys and research
22. Test market new products and services
23. Open new markets and territories
24. Support distributor and dealer push/pull programs
25. Increase your bottom-line profits

■ WHEN IS DIRECT RESPONSE BEST? ■

Jim Kobs, direct marketing pioneer and friend, introduced me to this concept: There are at least 8 situations when direct response is most likely to work and can be the best method to achieve your specific goal.

1. You Can Clearly Identify Your Target Audience

There are tens of thousands of mailing lists available. There are literally thousands of magazines and newspapers and hundreds of radio and television stations. Telephones are now common in most countries. And computers are fast becoming the communication tool of choice for much of the world. So, it is highly likely you will be able to target your audience clearly, identifying specifically the characteristics of the people and/or companies you wish to reach. If you can do this, direct response is an excellent tool.

2. You Can Reach Your Target Audience

It does no good to identify your audience on paper and then not reach them. It is easy to talk about people who have 2 jobs, but is there a list of them? Or is there a publication that reaches this group? What about the small office/home office (SOHO) audience? Many people fall into this category today and you can certainly talk about it. How do you reach this group?

Well, I'm not certain what you do to get to the 2-job folks. Today, it is much easier to reach the SOHO crowd through the press with industry-specific publications, the Web, and several direct mail lists.

Let's talk about both identifying *and* reaching your audience. Most of us would agree it's not too difficult to identify who we want to talk to. Yet, sometimes it is difficult to reach them.

An example of my own involves a major telephone company that had a product it felt would be of interest to people who moonlighted (i.e., worked 2 jobs, probably one full time and one part time). One group that fits this description is real estate agents. They are fairly easy to reach. Most must be licensed, and that information is usually public domain. Reaching real estate agents on behalf of this particular program was not difficult.

Another such audience is cabdrivers. Many drive nights and work at another job during the day or the reverse. However, have you ever heard of a list of cabdrivers? Even though they are licensed, we could find no public list of these drivers. Most work for companies or are part of a cooperative, still their names are not available. Further, we could not find a publication to reach them—there is no *Taxi Cab Journal* or *Taxi Cab News*. Basically, there was no direct way to reach cabdrivers.

What we did was take out ads in newspapers. Have you ever seen a cabdriver without a newspaper? Of course not. When they line up, they always have a newspaper. We thought it might work. It didn't! The newspaper was too broad a medium to be effective or efficient.

This is an example of why you must be able not only to clearly identify your marketplace (we could clearly identify cabdrivers), but also to reach them (as we did easily with the real estate agents).

3. You Have A Lot To Say About Your Product or Service

This also applies if your offering is expensive, unique, special, unusual, or new. Many times, a page in a magazine or 60 seconds of broadcast won't cut it. You need more space and/or more time. Direct response—making good use of direct mail, the telephone, and the World Wide Web—may allow you to tell your whole story. This also is possible with large-space newspaper advertisements—sometimes.

4. Your Product or Service Has Continuity, Repeat Sales

If you want to build a database of buyers or must do so to justify your promotional program, direct response is the way to go. Most successful businesses where direct marketing plays a role are built on repeat business and consumer sales. Sometimes you "buy" that initial sale, even at a loss, in order to gain a customer who, over time, will return a profit. Repeat sales play a major role in areas like consumables and supplies—anything that gets used up, such as office, computer, and medical supplies.

Hewlett Packard is a good example. The company's direct marketing division in northern California is an enormously successful operation, doing nothing but providing supplies, peripherals, add-ons, low-end software, and similar items to the installed base of Hewlett Packard users.

Every time you pick up a pencil or write on a yellow tablet, you are using a consumable that has to be replaced. Hospitals, clinics, and doctors' offices use bandages, syringes, and other supplies daily. They need to be replaced.

Direct response is an excellent way to sell products that fit the general description of "consumables."

5. You Need to Control the Entire Selling Message or Process

If you use an independent distribution system or network where the sales force (inside or outside) is not under your control, direct response can help. Those who sell business and consumer goods through wholesale, retail, or mail order are all excellent examples.

Selling through an independent network can be a challenge. All you can do is present your product and offer, and hope the dealers and distributors get excited. Hallmark Cards, Avery Label, Moore Business Forms, and many other companies use direct response marketing techniques to service and sell their dealer and distributor networks. IBM, MCI, and scores of other companies use direct response to sell direct to their customer base with a catalog, an inbound toll-free number, and an outbound telemarketing program.

The entire mail-order industry operates on the philosophy of controlling the selling message and process. A company named DEN-MAT, a dental supply firm headquartered in Santa Maria, California, services dentists on 3 continents with a catalog and an international toll-free number.

When your message must reach a specific audience and drive that person to a place (trade show, storefront, or your Web site), a telephone, or the mail box (with your order form, coupon, or reply card), direct response can work.

6. You Want to Build a Predictable, Repeatable Model

You are introducing a new product or service, or changing the position or image of a current product. You need a model you know can be repeated to achieve sales objectives. When Jack-in-the-Box and other restaurant chains introduce a new product, they build a marketing model. First, they select a small, representative group of stores. Next, they do a controlled mailing (a coupon offer) to their prospective customer base around those locations. The mailing tells the new product story and urges trial with a special offer. The chains then measure what happens. From the results, they get a predictable model that becomes the standard when rolling out to all locations. This same process is also used with outside dealer, distributor, and independent sales networks. The home office develops the program, tests it, and takes it to the field.

Direct response marketing is ideal under these conditions because it is:

- Action oriented
- Measurable
- Persuasive (makes the sale or leads to the sale)
- Repeatable

Companies as diverse as MicroAge Computer Stores, Safeco Insurance, and Der Weinerschnitzel all developed model programs this way.

7. Your Product or Service Doesn't Fit Other Distribution Channels

It isn't glamorous, it's too complicated, it doesn't sell itself, it needs lengthy explanation, it's too low priced—or maybe too high priced—to be interesting to other channels. So, you sell it direct.

An example of a product line that doesn't fit other distribution channels is low-end software, software costing under $100. The hundreds of computer stores that might carry a specific software package have literally thousands of software packages to select from. And because there are so many, they can't possibly carry them all. How do they decide?

Well, it's really rather easy. They select those that are going to be the hot sellers, that are relatively easy to explain, and that will make the store the most money. Most software costing less than $100, even though it may be easy to explain, does not offer much profit potential, making it a perfect product line for direct response.

The POWER UP! catalog is mailed several times a year to a targeted niche audience. The company has built a business that does in excess of a million dollars a month in software packages costing less than $100! Quite a story.

8. You Want Less Visibility in the Marketplace

You don't want to be seen nationally or even regionally yet. You are in a test situation: new market or product introduction, new SIC code, new geography, anything you want to test first and then roll. Direct marketing is an excellent testing discipline.

The offer is an important part of the success of any direct response marketing program and price is part of your offer. Cassette Productions Unlimited tested price when it introduced the album *Think and Grow Rich* by Napoleon Hill. Using direct mail, the company price tested $89.95 and $129.95 to determine, before it rolled out to a large marketplace through print and broadcast, what price would gain the most new customers and at least a satisfactory return on investment. Its business was expanding; Cassette Productions wanted a large, new customer base. Profits were important, yet new customers were more important if the company was to grow its mail-order business. For these and several other reasons, it selected the $89.95 price. This test helped management decide the direction to take.

ClubEarth, an environmental membership-based organization headquartered in British Columbia and working around the world, had a price "problem," too. Using the World Wide Web, it tested 3 price variations for each membership level—silver, gold, and platinum—before learning what combination worked best for its marketplace.

Direct response allows you to pinpoint specific markets and audiences in exact locations with special offers, and then gives you the measurability to take the next step.

■ MORE IDEAS ■

Glenmore Trenear-Harvey is a good friend from the United Kingdom and a true direct marketing professional. He has prepared a list of opportunities for which direct response could be the means to reach your goal. Here is a selection of those IDEAS:

- When you have an expensive storefront location
- When you have patchy distribution
- When you have a mail-order or information catalog
- When you have an outside sales force (yours or through a network of any type)
- If you run competitions or contests of any kind
- When you have a "family" of products
- When you are seeking trial or sampling
- When you have charge customers
- When you offer a guarantee/warranty/service contract
- When you have a very narrow marketplace
- When repeat business is the key to your success

- When you want to test anything for any reason (offer, market, new geography)
- If you have low-volume accounts
- When you are seeking to increase your customer base
- When you have large swings in sales patterns
- When you want to know which half of your advertising works

These ideas lay the groundwork for establishing a direct response marketing program. Now you have the basis for taking the first step in the process: thinking, planning, and organizing (the hard part!).

▪ THE MARKETING PLAN PLAN ▪

I am sold on the writing of sound marketing plans. When I say that I mean a plan that assembles into one spot all the vital up-to-date information on the product, so that when the whole picture is spread before me, the indicated course of action becomes clearly a sound procedure.

Clarence Eldridge
Vice President, Marketing
Campbell Soup Company

I agree with Mr. Eldridge. He is right in his evaluation that a marketing plan—a process of thinking before action—is needed.

Planning is essential because, as Lloyd S. Nelson of the NASA Corporation said: "If they can do it next year with no plan, why didn't they do it last year?" Seat-of-the-pants marketing programs rarely achieve success. Yes, periodically there is a unique "fad" that is truly a success. The pet rock story of the 1980s, Beanie Babies (stuffed animals) in the late 1990s, and hula hoops from way back come to mind.

For most of us planning is vital. The Marketing Plan Plan is a 19-point checklist of things to consider as you begin the process of establishing your direct response marketing program. It is divided into 4 parts:

1. The facts
2. The situation
3. Strategy and tactics
4. The method

Let's walk through each of these parts one by one.

The Facts

There's an old saying that your decisions are no better than your facts. Facts and ideas are the lifeblood of sound marketing. Without facts, ideas can be meaningless—and vice versa.

At this stage, you will want to summarize the most important points, the facts as they are applicable to your product or service in your marketplace. You want all the information you can get. Pinpoint this information as either problems that need to be overcome or circumvented or as opportunities to be taken advantage of. In addition, this section should contain a statement of your company goals, as far as this special product is concerned.

The following summary of items is designed as a checklist for your planning process. Details of the process are covered in Chapters 2 through 9.

Gather All Necessary Background Information
- A brief marketing and sales history
- A review of where you have been
- A summary of where you are now
- A further statement on where you want to go
- Information on the size and scope of your marketplace
- Details on pricing history and gross profit history
- What share of the market you own today
- What share of the market your leading competitor has
- A summary of any company resources and cultural climate that may be important to achieving your goal

Identify Specific Problems and Opportunities for Your Services

- □ What are your strengths?
- □ What are your weaknesses?
- □ Does your company have the resources and commitment necessary for success?
- □ What are you doing now that's working?
- □ What are you doing now that's not working?
- □ What did you do in the past that worked but you've stopped doing it?
- □ What would make you more efficient?
- □ What is getting in the way of your success?

Draw Your Overall Direction Conclusions Based on the Facts You've Gathered

- □ What business are you in?
- □ What business should you be in?
- □ What should your short-term objectives be?
- □ What results do you expect from your present way of doing things?
- □ How do you get to where you want to go from where you are?

To be successful, you must at least think about and come to some conclusion about each of these questions. You may elect to skip one that may not be applicable, but at least consider all of them so you know what you're doing.

Once you've accomplished this evaluation, you can begin your marketing process around a structured framework.

The Situation

You have gathered some facts. Now, what do they mean? How do you evaluate what you have gathered? What do you do with the facts given the market situation?

You objectively look at your product or service, your marketplace, the competition, and distribution channel options; that is, you fully and completely evaluate where you are. To continue with the checklist, here are the next 7 points.

Clear Product Identification

Not only must you know what business you're in, you must know your product.

- What products and services do you offer?
- Can you promote this product to a significant portion of existing customers?
- Does the product lend itself to sale by mail order, or would lead generation or traffic building be better?
- Does this product have the potential for large sales *and* profits?
- How and where does it fit into your profit grid?
- Can the product attract new customers?
- Does it take advantage of your existing strengths?
- Where does it fit among all similar offerings in the marketplace?

Clear Market Identification

- Market identification means people.
- Market identification means companies.
- Market identification means geography.
- Market identification means social, cultural, technical, economic, political, and environmental factors—both positive and negative.
- Market identification means knowing the demand for this product in your area.
- Market identification means knowing if you have the ability to be the leader in this field.

Competition Evaluation and Understanding

- What is the level of the competition? Where do you fit among the competition?

- What are the current strengths and weaknesses of your primary competition?
- What is the competition doing now?
- What are the probable future actions of your competitors?
- What can you do NOW to take advantage of your competition?

Consideration of All Communication Options

Image advertising does not work . . . alone. Except for new product introduction there was no discernible correlation between advertising weight and sales levels. . . . Image advertising needed the impact of sales promotion, events, POP, and direct mail.

> Valerie H. Free
> Publisher
> *Marketing Communications*

Sadly, *Marketing Communications* as a publication is dead and gone. Yet, this quote from Ms. Free is still valid as we do direct marketing in the 21st century. If there is anything marketing has learned from advertising, it is the value of multimedia—using more than one tool to reach your marketplace, make your offer, and achieve your objective.

These are the media tools to be considered as you plan an integrated direct marketing program:

- Sales promotion
- Point-of-purchase displays
- Package inserts
- Postcard decks
- Direct mail
- Catalogs
- Direct response print (newspapers and magazines)
- Public relations
- Video and film
- Advertising specials and premiums
- Collateral and sales support materials

- Trade shows
- Telemarketing
- Direct response broadcast (radio and television)
- The World Wide Web

You need to make an open-minded review of the variety of communication options available. Don't eliminate anything until you've completed the entire planning process.

Real Customer/User Purchase Decision Habits

There are always 3 types of people involved with every decision, in the home as well as at the office:

- The *user* of the product or service.
- The *influencer*, who is usually someone of more importance than the user. In business, it could even be somebody in another department.
- The *decision maker*, who is usually somebody at an even higher level. In business, it is someone from upper-middle or upper management.

In addition to these 3 people, you may need to weave your way through several others. In the business marketplace, this can include a buyer, a purchasing agent, or a financial officer (someone who gives you the order).

Maybe the idea for this buying decision comes from another party entirely: the husband for the wife, the wife for the kids, the kids for the family. Sometimes this person is called an *initiator*. In business, this could be someone outside the immediate area of responsibility, someone who sees a benefit in a product or service and urges a buy. They have no authority, yet they could very well get the process rolling by raising the question and kicking the door open.

In other cases, you may have a *gatekeeper*, someone who protects the person you want to reach. This happens at home as well as in the office. At home, it could be a woman protecting her children or husband. In the office, this person may have the title of executive secretary or administrative assistant. He or she has the responsibility for screening you out.

In any instance, you need to understand the decision habits of the real customer (the user/purchaser).

Sales Force/Distribution Methods

How are you going to distribute your product? Through which channels? Your methods could include:

- An in-house order desk
- An outbound telemarketing unit
- Outside independent sales reps
- A captive sales force
- A network, such as dealers or distributors
- An in-house retail sales force
- The World Wide Web
- A part of customer service
- A mix of any of these

Before you determine *how* you are going to sell, you must clearly identify which channels offer you the most opportunity for success. Please note I'm using the plural—channels, as in more than one.

- What is the sales history of each channel type?
- What does your competition do (how do they distribute)?
- What are the buying habits and attitudes of the principal channels under consideration?
- Where can you promote the most effectively?
- What is happening in your marketplace industrywide?

Overall Company Positioning

Consider not only your positioning, but awareness and image factors, and suspect/prospect/customer audience perception.

- What position do you currently own in your marketplace?
- What position do you want to own in your marketplace?

▫ Do you have to beat the leader to get the position you want?

▫ Do you have the resources (money/staff/commitment) to achieve the position you want?

▫ Can you take the time it will take to gain the position you want?

▫ Do your current position and the one you want to have match?

In order to achieve the company positioning you want, your position must be:

- Important to your audience
- Unique for your audience
- Believable to your audience
- Deliverable to your audience

Put these specific details on paper first. Then and only then are you ready to establish your strategy and create the tactics to make it happen.

The Strategy and Tactics

Let's define our terms. Strategy equals planning. *Strategies* are planned actions designed to reach objectives. Tactics equal doing the plan. *Tactics* are the details of how you will achieve your plan. To use a military analogy, strategy or planning is concerned with the broad outlook—the total picture of what is to come. Tactics, or the doing part, are the very specific maneuvers that make the plan happen and bring it to life.

This is true for both the short-range and the long-range planning necessary to achieve your corporate goals. Here is where the planning process begins in earnest. Even brilliant tactics, with the finest copy and the best graphics, cannot save a program that is strategically weak. You must do the planning first! Strategy comes from people and their experiences. It comes from that tough process of THINKING.

This is *really* how you do power direct marketing right. You begin by thinking and planning.

Describe Your Specific Marketing Objectives

In most cases, you will have more than a single objective for your direct marketing plan. Make sure you put them in priority order. Undoubtedly, you will have a master objective. At the same time, each medium will have its own objective. Set them accordingly.

Marketing and sales must work together. Marketing comes first; its purpose is to fuel sales. So, as each sales channel will have a sales target, marketing needs to be conceived with this knowledge. All objectives need to be set in harmony with marketing and sales.

Outline a Strategy to Reach These Objectives

Your overall strategy includes the courses of action you will take to achieve your objectives for each product or service, including pricing, promotion, and fulfillment.

Decide on the Message and Various Media

From the various communication options outlined in "The Situation" section, select those most adaptable to your specific needs. Then begin the creative and media planning process to relay your message as an integrated marketing program.

Determine the Tactics to Support Your Objectives

The purpose of tactics is to work within the strategies you have set to achieve your objectives. They do not function independently, nor are they developed to win awards. Remember, more than one tactic can be used to achieve a specific point in your plan.

Budget to Make It All Happen

There is no such thing as a free lunch! Establish a budget for the strategies you have outlined and the tactics you have chosen to achieve your objectives.

Assign a Timetable and Schedule

Planning requires a long-range focus—a thinking timeframe. Not tomorrow or next week, not a knee-jerk reaction, but fiscal and calendar-year planning for maybe as long as 2 years.

I do not believe in 5-year plans for marketing. Why? Because in the 74 years from 1917 to 1991, the leaders of what we knew in the West as the USSR did not once make their 5-year plan work. It was never anything more than a paper-pushing exercise. That is not the only reason, but it is a reason.

The real "why" is because the marketplace is moving so fast that anything beyond a year or 2 is pure fantasy. Direct response timetables for a complete plan usually cover 4 to 12 months. Determine how much time, including contingencies, you need to accomplish your objectives and then schedule accordingly.

Develop a Measurement/Analysis System

Determine early on how you will measure the effectiveness (or lack thereof) of your direct marketing program. Measurement occurs following the implementation of the tactics. Yet, planning for measurement must be done in the beginning, as your objectives are being set. Strategy is planning—planning how you will best utilize your resources of time, money, facilities, and, most importantly, people to achieve your objectives.

Your plan is now on paper, ready to happen. As Eisenhower said: "Planning is everything. The plan is nothing." Making it happen is why you do it all in the first place.

The Method

"Do you want me to plan it . . . or do it?" Have you heard that before? Sure, everyone has at one time or another. It's natural under the fire of day-to-day activity.

The direct response marketing plan is a comprehensive, detailed written document. It identifies in concrete terms the thoughts and corresponding direct response tactics needed to achieve and fulfill the plan.

Those responsible for all areas of marketing and the marketing mix should work together. The team, or "The Group" as Richard Shaver likes to call them, includes the full marketing service and creative team, sales, and management. It also might include representatives from finance, manufacturing, administration, data processing, and maybe R&D.

It is in this area where the greatest cooperation and closest coordination are essential. Putting the plan together is not a project for an individual—it is a company effort. It is now time to put the details of your plan to work, to develop the program.

What promotional material, advertising specialties, advertising, merchandising, public relations, sales promotion, and direct marketing is needed to tell your story? How can you tell it so the entire marketing effort moves in one direction at the same time and is effective?

Prepare Creative to Accomplish Your Objectives
The key word here is "your." You know what your direction is, or you should before you get to the creative part of the plan. You answered the necessary questions earlier:

- Where have you been?
- Where are you now?
- Where are you going?

The creative team must know your focus as clearly as management and marketing do. Know your direction. Know your goals. Know your objectives. You will then be able to aim your creative team toward getting you where you are going.

Produce the Program and Take It to the Marketplace
At General Foods we don't have what are usually referred to as advertising plans. Instead we have marketing plans . . . to get the maximum efficiency out of our marketing expenditures. We believe that advertising and selling and all the corollary functions of marketing should have a common objective. The

annual marketing plan is the means by which we arrive at these common objectives.

Edwin W. Ebel

Vice President, Marketing

General Foods Corporation

Aristotle thought an unplanned life was not very productive because individuals didn't know where they were or what they were trying to do. They didn't know where they were going or how to get there. The same philosophy is applicable to direct marketing.

■ The 8ight Point Market Action Plan —an Introduction ■

The Marketing Plan Plan is based on a paper from the 3M Corporation, London, Ontario. Several years ago, I enjoyed the opportunity of working with 3M-Canada, one of the more innovative manufacturing organizations in the world, offering over 65,000 products. Because 3M is very much an entrepreneurship-type company, many of its best ideas come from its own people. I mention this because 3M deserves credit for this plan. Working with such an outstanding organization taught me a lot.

Even though I firmly believe my Marketing Plan Plan is an ideal guide toward building a direct response marketing plan, it is too much to work with. Why? Because, in my experience of getting companies of all sizes to consider planning, the overwhelming detail of the Marketing Plan Plan is too much to swallow—at least at one time.

So, using the original plan as a foundation, I distilled the knowledge, overlaid my experience, and created *The 8ight Point Market Action Plan*. With just 8 easy-to-remember phrases, this plan serves as a platform to think, plan, organize, and then develop and create an effective direct response marketing plan (see Figure 1.2).

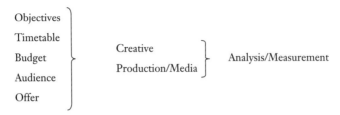

Figure 1.2 ■ The 8ight Point Market Action Plan

Always remember the importance of planning. Lee Iacocca said:

We are, it seems, deeply prejudiced against planning, especially against large-scale planning or planning that looks
beyond the immediate future or the short-term advantage.
Economic or industrial planning has, quite falsely and
simplistically, become associated in our minds with social-
ist systems and thus with inefficient and unresponsive
bureaucracies.

The lesson we must draw from the failure of such planning is not that planning itself is bad, but that bad planning
is bad. Those who feel that planning of any kind is alien to
the capitalist system should consider where IBM, Honda,
and a hundred other successful businesses would be today if
they had not committed themselves to sound planning.

It has been my experience that any organization that
does not take planning seriously does not take thinking seriously. They go together and cannot be separated. Or, as that
apparently simple but profound saying puts it: "If you don't
know where you are going, any road will take you there."
The only way we are going to cope with change and com-
plexity is through effective planning.

In order to plan effectively, you have to know where you're
going. Abraham Lincoln was a man who knew where he was going.
He missed no opportunity to sell voters on his candidacy for Congress. In 1846, Lincoln attended a preaching service of his opponent,

a circuit riding preacher named Peter Cartwright. Cartwright called on all who wished to go to heaven to stand up. Everyone rose except Lincoln. Then Cartwright called for all who did not want to go to hell to rise. Again, everyone rose except Lincoln. Cartwright said, "I am grieved to see Abe Lincoln sitting back there unmoved by these appeals. If he doesn't want to go to heaven and doesn't want to escape hell, will he tell us where he does want to go?"

Lincoln rose and slowly said, "I'm going to Congress." Lincoln won the election. He knew where he was going.

The 8ight Point Market Action Plan is a basic formula, an idea plan. You use it to establish, create, develop, and implement a direct marketing plan for any product or any service. It will help you get where you're going.

For maximum effectiveness, The 8ight Point Plan calls for a closely knit working partnership. This is to ensure that all areas of the marketing, sales, and advertising process are finely attuned to your sales objectives so you get where you're going.

For your direct marketing program to be successful, the following four things must happen.

1. *Management* needs to make a commitment. A commitment, not a simple statement of "We'll try this." A commitment is necessary in order to give each new program a full opportunity to work. Did you learn to ride a bicycle the first time you got on it or to type the first time you sat at a keyboard? Rarely do we succeed the first time we try anything new or achieve maximum success when we take our first steps to improve what we're already doing. A full commitment from management is necessary for your direct response program to succeed.

2. *Marketing* needs to make a commitment. This is usually not a serious problem, except where the responsibility is given to those who think direct marketing equals direct mail (they don't understand the discipline and are not interested in learning). In most cases, marketing has a charge to achieve and is willing to commit to the task.

3. *Sales* needs to make a commitment. This is more important than a commitment from management, because if everything else

works and salespeople decide this is something they don't care for, the program will fail. Any excuse (rarely a reason) will do: "The leads are no good." "I already know my territory." "No one likes junk mail." "I don't like getting calls during dinner and know my customers don't either." You name it and sales can find a reason not to. Having sold since age 12 when my dad tossed me out the door with the charge to do just that, I can relate. You probably can, too. So, early in the planning process get the sales team aboard.

4. *Everyone* has to work together. Which means that each unit—management, marketing, and sales—must work together from the beginning. This is not a single-meeting process. It will take a number of visits and exchanges, reviews and considerations, plus some give-and-take to come to the bottom line. This requires management, marketing, and sales working together as a team.

In my experience, the programs that are the most successful are those where a total commitment from all 3 groups is planned from the beginning. Keyword Office Technologies, a high-tech firm with headquarters in Calgary, Alberta; Wells Fargo Bank of Oakland, California; MicroAge Computer Stores of Tempe, Arizona (a franchise operation with hundreds of locations); Canada Post Corporation in Ottawa, Ontario; and Krames Communications, a business-to-business mail-order education company in the medical field, in San Bruno, California—they've each had smashingly successful direct response marketing programs because they got the team together early on. It works!

The 8ight Point Market Action Plan was developed to provide you with the information necessary to produce outstanding marketing programs that are properly focused and directed, highly effective and efficient. The plan covers the areas of knowledge essential to establish a profitable and successful program for your needs.

Chapter 2

OBJECTIVES

Ready, Aim, Fire—Marketing by Objectives

■ ■ ■

Client Marco Brown of Wells Fargo Bank introduced me to the 6 phases of a project (see Figure 2.1). I thought you would enjoy them, too. Because if you're alive and well and have been active in sales, marketing, advertising, public relations, or sales promotion, this process has undoubtedly happened to you at least once—probably more often.

In order to avoid this type of thinking, I've built The 8ight Point Market Action Plan, introduced in Chapter 1. This step-by-step process guides you through the think, plan, organize, develop, do, and measure parts of a direct response marketing program. Here, again, are the 8 points to the plan:

- Objectives
- Timetable
- Budget
- Audience
- Offer
- Creative

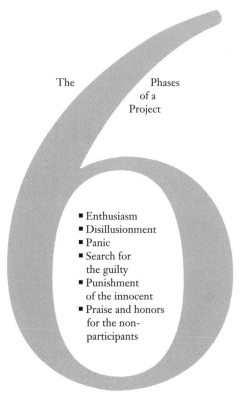

The Phases of a Project

- Enthusiasm
- Disillusionment
- Panic
- Search for the guilty
- Punishment of the innocent
- Praise and honors for the non-participants

Figure 2.1 The 6 Phases of a Project

- Production/Media
- Analysis/Measurement

Or, as Kenneth Blanchard said: "Don't just do something. Think about it."

R. C. Cunningham, executive vice president of AFG Industries, says it this way:

Every company has the opportunity to minimize head-on competition and to maximize their sales and profit potential by hitting 'em where they ain't. The key to finding where they ain't is a well-defined strategic plan which . . . evaluates the strengths and weaknesses of your company compared with the competition.

This information . . . becomes the road map that tells you where you are today, lets you see where you want to go tomorrow and how to get there. It's really knowing your market, and your competition, that makes the difference in selling a commodity product, a high-tech product, or a multimillion dollar piece of equipment successfully.

■ FOCUS, DIRECTION, AND SETTING OBJECTIVES ■

Objectives is the first point of The 8ight Point Market Action Plan. You need objectives. I need objectives. A company needs objectives. Focus and direction come as the result of setting specific objectives. And from objectives come accomplishment. Things get done because a plan is in place to do something.

Objectives provide a feeling of progress. They serve to reduce the wandering-about approach to achieving your goals and the shoot-from-the-hip philosophy.

Having objectives eliminates the "reaction to the current situation" practice far too many companies use as a method for setting direction. Initiating activities in response to marketplace activity is a way of becoming just like the rest of the pack. Having objectives helps you get from where you are to where you need to be without being sidetracked.

At DuPont, each communications manager has the responsibility of providing a "direction sheet" at the start of each new project. This sheet provides focus and direction for that particular program. The purpose is to be very specific with information so the creative group will know what is expected. Here are some of the questions addressed and answered:

- What is the product? What are the features and benefits of this product?

- What is the marketing purpose of this program? What do we want and expect to happen? What are the objectives?
- Who is the target audience? Who are we talking to?
- What are the needs of this audience?
- What is the SINGLE, most important IDEA to convey?
- What are the other copy points in order of importance?
- What do we want the reader to do? What type of action is requested?
- What is the timing for all of this?
- What is the budget?

If appropriate, additional information on any ideas for media and creative direction, graphic, copy, and legal requirements are provided. The plan to measure results and supporting details about the competition, distribution, and sales all might be included. This gives a very complete overview with focus and direction. A good way to do business.

Few people would question the necessity of setting goals in marketing, if for no other reason than to avoid the "Ready, Fire, Aim" possibility. What's negative about Ready, Fire, Aim? If you're making a good offer to a specific marketplace, why not just do it? For the same reason a rocket shot to the moon must be heading in the right direction when it leaves Earth—you must have your objectives in order before you jump into the marketplace. Without direction you're likely to end up someplace other than where you intended!

With the sophisticated technology available today it is possible to push buttons and pull levers here on Earth to change the direction of a rocket in space, alter its trajectory around the Earth, turn cameras on and off, even land on the moon or another planet and return to Earth. *But only because the rocket was heading in the right direction from the start.*

Ditto for direct marketing objectives. Once you set them, you can change or alter them; improve, eliminate, or add to them. But only when you're heading in the right direction from the beginning.

Your objectives must be:

- Brief enough to be understood
- Clear enough to be acted upon
- Flexible enough to allow adaptation to the circumstances

Only when you've planned your program thoroughly will you truly be in a Ready, Aim, Fire mode.

Most of us recognize the value of planning, of setting objectives, of plotting a direction. However, there is more involved with this process than many believe or wish to take the time to learn and implement.

Here are some key questions to ask—and answer—as you set objectives for your company, your product, and your service:

1. Does your company offer a discernible advantage over what is available from the competition?
2. Is your company's advantage important to the market? Does the market know or care?
3. Does your product or service offer a distinct advantage?
4. Is this advantage important to the market?
5. Are you the industry follower or the industry leader?
6. Are you a new entry with this product? In this market?
7. Are you aggressively aiming to take business from the competition?
8. Can you withstand retaliation to your approach (can you take the heat)?

Before any marketing or advertising program is begun, most people have a basic idea of what they want to achieve. Yet, many times goals are expressed in rather vague terms which may be a mix of overall corporate, marketing, and advertising objectives. For example, an objective "to increase sales" is not particularly useful. By how much do you want to increase sales? In which specific product areas? Everywhere, or only in certain geographic regions?

Your objectives must be defined, documented, specific, and numeric. You may want to set objectives to achieve goals such as the following:

- Realize a specific percentage of market share or market penetration—as long as you can translate the percentage to money in sales and in profits
- Raise a level of sales turnover by product or product group
- Achieve a set number of new accounts within a specific time frame
- Revive a specific number of accounts over the coming calendar year
- Break into new SIC business codes during the next fiscal year
- Get into a set number of new geographic marketplaces (expand your reach)
- Establish a rate of financial growth from current customers

It is important to quantify your objectives. When goals are not defined in specific terms, it is nearly impossible to measure performance. And in direct marketing, "If you can't measure it, you can't improve it," according to Alex d'Arbeloff, president of Teradyne.

YOU must set your objectives, define your goals, determine what you want to achieve. No one from outside your company can begin to decide what your objectives should be. Only you can do that all-important task.

Why do I state so strongly you must be responsible for setting your objectives? Why do I suggest that to do otherwise is unwise? Because nearly every time I have helped set objectives for a company, the plan failed to materialize. In the few instances where a plan was begun, it was never finished. The reason? I think it was because there was no blood, sweat, and tears in the effort. It is folly to think anyone from outside your organization can tell those inside what your goals ought to be. That's what objectives are—goals. Specifics to accomplish, mountains to climb, rivers to cross. How can anyone—even I—tell you what your marketing goals for the next year should be? Objectives must be set by those persons who have the responsibility to make them happen.

▪ SOME QUESTIONS TO CONSIDER ▪

Here are some questions for you to consider as you plan your direct marketing program objectives:

1. What are your projected sales revenues for the short term and the long term? What are you looking for, and what is acceptable?
2. What are your revenue goals by individual product or product group? Do you have different objectives for different geographic regions?
3. What is your target cost per sales lead and per sales close?
4. What is your sales pattern locally, regionally, nationally, and internationally? Can you coattail your advertising to gain more results? Is there a seasonal pattern that you know must be addressed?
5. Are there any legal or other marketing restrictions you know will affect your plans? Can you work around them?
6. What is the industry history, your corporate history, and the sales trend or direction for the past 2 years? Is the marketplace action similar to this time last year, or is it different? How?
7. What is your advertising/marketing history for the past 2 years? Did you meet your sales objectives, fall short, or surpass your plan?

▪ THE 9-BOX MATRIX ▪

You may recall from your university days and Marketing 101 the simple 9-Box Matrix. If you, like me, need a memory jogger, see

PRODUCTS

	Existing	Modified	New
New	1	2	3
Expanded	4	5	6
Existing	7	8	9

MARKETS

Figure 2.2 ■ The 9-Box Matrix

Figure 2.2. Markets are read vertically, products horizontally. A new product aimed at a new market goes in box 3. An existing product directed toward an expanded market is in box 4. A modified product at an existing market is in box 8.

A key element in setting good objectives is to determine for each of the various products, product lines, and services you offer, in which box that particular offer fits. The primary reason you set objectives is to have focus and direction, the thought being that they will translate into sales—and PROFITS!

Different products and services at different stages of their life cycles have different opportunities in the marketplace. If it has been around awhile, is a commodity item, is at a mature stage, and/or has intense competition, the product offers you much less opportunity for increased profit. On the other hand, a new product, an enhanced product, or an opening in a new market (either by geography or type of audience) may offer you greatly increased sales and profit options.

The 9-Box Matrix raises such questions as:

- What do we make that could be modified to become another product?
- Can we modify our products to make them work better in new applications?
- Could we simply reposition a product to serve new markets?
- Is it possible to locate expanded markets for our existing products?
- Is it possible to locate new markets for modified products (bundled or unbundled)?
- Are we taking a new product to a new marketplace during the coming year?
- Are we taking a new product to one of our existing marketplaces?
- Could we sell products differently (for example, by mail-order catalog sales) in addition to the existing channels?

Your answers to the questions applicable to your company's products and services, as well as where your product fits in the 9-Box Matrix, will determine how you set your marketing objectives.

It's easy to take something new to a new marketplace. The chart is clear. You accordingly set objectives to achieve, a timetable for doing so, and a new product introduction budget.

It's tougher with existing products and services. Sure, you know what you did last year and the year before. You also have a feel for your competitors, what they're doing. You have established a position and created an image. You know your awareness levels. You know how to generate interest in what you have to offer. You've already invested in educating the marketplace. Now all you need to do is SELL THE PRODUCT AT A REASONABLE PROFIT. And, depending on all factors, you will determine where in the 9-Box Matrix your objective standards will be set. You will decide how much time and money should be allocated to that product line to achieve your objectives, what its bottom-line worth will be to you, how much you can invest to get the return you need and want.

In most cases, you will benefit by setting your objectives with the pace of change in mind. In today's world, things move quickly. You need to be flexible to your customers' and prospects' wants, desires, and (most importantly) NEEDS. At the same time, using the fast-paced market as an "excuse" not to set objectives is just that—an excuse. Don't fall for that line. Instead, commit to setting objectives and working at making them happen.

■ How to Develop Good Objectives ■

How do you set good objectives? Here is a 6-point plan.

Good Objectives Must Be Specific

You need specific statements about the results you are seeking. Specific means numeric, not percentages. Why? Have you ever cheated using percentages? Sure, join the crowd. Everyone has. I learned how to cheat using percentages from my dad. He didn't know he taught me, but he did. Dad was an active board member at the local Methodist church. One evening he came home and said, "The board wants us to tithe. Is that 10 percent before taxes or after?"

Because it is so easy to "manage" percentages, using them to set objectives allows for a way out. You really don't want that to happen. Real, live numbers are facts. Percentages are generic. Use real numbers to set your objectives. Be specific.

Good Objectives Must Be Measurable

Measurable means you can count your results. You can measure your level of success or lack thereof.

Remember that "more" only sets the direction—it is not specific and thus cannot be measured. It does not include the qualifiers of when and how far, both of which are necessary for measurable objectives.

You want to be able to measure each of the following:

- Number of units sold
- Rate of return on your investment
- Cost-to-sales ratio
- Market share
- Money (the real measure!)

If your objectives are specific, they allow for honest measurement. You will know what happened, for better or worse, which is important now and next time.

Make your objectives measurable.

Good Objectives Must Be Realistic

You should set tough standards, reach for the stars, stand on your toes. At the same time, you don't want your objectives to be so tough a 1-year goal takes 16 months to achieve. Nor do you want them so easy you've accomplished your yearly objectives by April.

Only experience and common sense allow you to be realistic. Automatically increasing your objectives by a set percentage from year to year, without consideration for the life cycle of the product, is not fair or realistic.

Setting objectives forces you to consider your resources to carry them out—resources such as personnel, time, technology, and money.

Set challenging and realistic objectives.

Good Objectives Must Have a Schedule

I've never had a program without a timetable. If there is ever a problem, it is that insufficient time is scheduled to accomplish what needs to be done. Sometimes not enough time has been allowed to develop a program, to think through the best course of action, to really take the time to plan what to do.

Many times, there has been adequate time to develop and implement a program. On paper it looks great. Then something slips—and then something else. Pretty soon you're behind schedule and people at the end of the line get pushed to the limit, even too far.

✐ Having good objectives means setting reasonable schedules and following them through the entire campaign.

Good Objectives Are Compatible with Everything Else in Your Organization

Because direct marketing is new in some circles, it is exciting. Some companies look at direct response as *the* answer to their problems. It scratches the itch.

This is all well and good. Yet, before you destroy what you already have going, test all new programs. Set your objectives in such a way that you can weave them into the fabric of your company's operations, not change everything. Good objectives are compatible with all plans.

Good Objectives Must Be Written

There are a number of reasons you put your objectives in writing. One reason is it gives you a reference guide. Another is it allows others you are working with to have full knowledge of where you're coming from and where you are going.

Again, I've never seen a marketing plan, or even a small project, where the objectives were not in writing. We know that must happen.

I do recommend you write them in "pencil," because you will change something. Know that you will change because the marketplace will change. Your competition will introduce an enhancement. Your company will come out with a new product (early or late, it doesn't matter—it requires a change).

```
S  =  Specific
M  =  Measurable
A  =  Attainable
R  =  Realistic
T  =  Time-Bound
```

Figure 2.3 ■ The SMART Method

Good objectives are in writing, so you can be flexible. The Wrangler division of Blue Bell sets its product marketing objectives by the SMART method, which you may find helpful in remembering the key points in setting good objectives (see Figure 2.3).

■ SOME DIRECT MARKETING OBJECTIVES ■

Here are some examples of good, specific direct marketing objectives:

- For a nationwide sales organization—To get 2 new leads per week, each week of the current fiscal year, for each outside sales representative.
- For a fast-food restaurant—To increase the frequency of visits and average ticket sale from its best customers from 5 to 6 visits per month, and from $3.23 per ticket to $3.65 per ticket.
- For a fund-raising organization—To increase the average donation from all donors who have previously given a minimum of $25 to an average of $35.
- For a sales organization with an independent dealer/distributor network—To generate 2,000 leads per month, of which a minimum of 500 will be highly qualified as "passionate" or "hot," thus requiring a sales rep visit and a demonstration of a new product.

■ For a mail-order company—To increase the average order frequency and average dollar amount from its best customer list from 4 times to 5 times a year, and from $37.50 per order to $45.00.

The first point of The 8ight Point Market Action Plan is Objectives. This is the foundation for all that follows. Without soundly thought-out and planned objectives, you have no direction. You have no focus. You will do marketing by wandering about. You *must* have objectives if you're to achieve your goals.

H. L. Hunt summed it up as well as anyone. He said:

1. Decide what you want to do, set your objectives.
2. Decide what you'll give up to get those objectives.
3. Decide your priorities as they relate to all you want or need to do against those objectives.
4. Get on about your work!

This is how power direct marketing works. Begin by marketing by objectives.

Chapter 3

TIMETABLE

EVERYTHING TAKES LONGER THAN IT TAKES

■ ■ ■

The 90/90 Law of Work Schedules says the first 90% of the job takes the first 90% of the time. The last 10% of the job takes the other 90% of the time. This is one of Murphy's Laws—and so true.

Timetable is the second point of The 8ight Point Plan. It has 2 parts:

1. The best time to be in the marketplace
2. The schedule—how to plan a full direct response program, probably a multimedia effort, certainly with a repeated series of messages

■ WHEN TO MAIL ■

The Direct Marketing Association has charted direct mail response by months (year-end holiday gift offerings excluded). Generally, it is a reliable guide for any mail project. Here's how you read this table. If your mailer gets 100 replies in January, the same offer to the same list presented with the same direct mail package will get 67 responses in June and 81 in November.

Month	Comparative Response
January	100.0%
February	96.3
March	71.0
April	71.5
May	71.5
June	67.0
July	73.3
August	87.0
September	79.0
October	89.9
November	81.0
December	79.0

As part of an extensive survey on direct mail response, *Catalog Age* prepared the chart shown in Figure 3.1. Generally speaking, across all combined categories (business and consumer), and for all product groups, catalogers found September and October to be the best months to mail. January was a close runner-up.

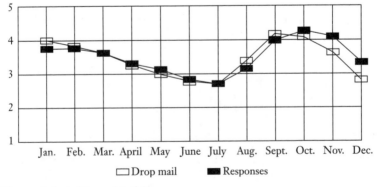

Figure 3.1 ■ Direct Mail Response

When *Is* the Best Time?

This time, like all times, is a very good one, if we but know what to do with it.

Emerson

Okay, when is the best time for you? It depends on your product and your marketplace. Is the product for consumers, you and me at home? Or is your offer directed toward businesses?

Business and industry direct marketers usually don't have the same seasonality as do consumer organizations, although this is not always the case. For several years, I sold Christmas trees and holiday decorations to large companies, office buildings, hotels, and the like. Try that in July if you feel season doesn't matter.

For the most part companies that sell business-to-business have to do it year-round. Yes, there may be one "season" that is better than another, maybe even 2 seasons. For example, fashion has 2 distinct buying seasons. The telecommunications and computer industries also make major new product announcements at key trade shows twice a year. All their promotions are tied to these major special events.

Almost every month, there is a holiday—January has New Year's Day; February 14 is Valentine's Day for most of the world; March has St. Patrick's Day; and all types of religious holidays fill out the year. It goes on and on like this. Different countries have different holidays. And almost every month, everywhere, something special is happening.

None of this is going to change. At least, neither you nor I are going to change it anytime soon. So, if you tie your marketing programs to special events, holidays, and other occasions, you have to be alert to timing.

This is equally true for both business and consumer marketers. If you are American Greetings and sell cards and gifts for special days, you must sell-in to your dealers months ahead. If, like Baskin-Robbins, you take advantage of special days for special promotions, you must sign up your network of dealer stores or distributors months ahead. Baskin-Robbins works as much as 9 months ahead in arranging its promotional calendar.

Many products can be sold at almost any time. Books are a good example. Although the chart may show some ups and downs in book sales, the range from best to worse is slight. Telephone products move at a fairly steady flow every month. Anything that can be classified as a consumable, a commodity, or supplies is sold on a rather even keel month after month.

Timing is important for companies that offer certain financial products. In the United States, you may fund your individual retirement account anytime during the year, up to April 15 of the following year, tax time. When do most Americans fund theirs? In the 45 days immediately before the absolute deadline. How far in advance do you do your birthday, anniversary, graduation, or holiday gift buying? Scores of thousands do it at the very last minute—even though they have months of prior notice.

If you use the telephone as a selling tool, you may find some research summarized in *The Mouser Report* interesting. Researchers analyzed 25,000 calls to consumers at home, weekdays only, from 8:00 A.M. to 9:00 P.M. Here's what they found:

- The best months to call are December and January (certainly not a surprise).
- The best days are Monday and Tuesday.
- More calls will be answered in rural areas (again, no surprise here).
- 20% of the time the line will be out of order (a large number!).
- 2% of the time the line will be busy (only 2%?).
- 29% of the time an eligible adult will not be home (believable).
- 24% of all calls won't be answered.
- 10% of all calls will reach an eligible person (not very often).
- 15% of those answering will refuse to talk.

What does all this say? I think it says almost anytime is a good time. Sure, some times will be better than others. When you plan well in advance you can conduct your promotion at the time you choose.

A friend from Australia tells a story about how Time-Life Books found a "new" selling season. With the seasons reversed from those in the Northern Hemisphere, the year-end religious and New Year holidays are in the middle of the summer Down Under. School is out, and many are on vacation. It was traditional to NOT do any new product offerings at this time. They were bound to fail because no one was at home, right? Wrong! The weeks between December 26 and January 31 became one of the best selling seasons for Time-Life because it elected to try something that "everyone" said would fail. And guess what—it worked! You could find a similar season for your product.

The short and long of this is that any time may be the time for you. The business world doesn't stop, ever—at most, it slows down.

When families with kids go on vacation, the rest of the world is home. You must pick what appears to be your logically best time and test. You may find any time is good; some times are just better than others.

Some Questions to Consider

What are some of the things you should consider in deciding when to be in the marketplace? The following questions can help:

- What is your competition up to? If they are active and you are not, you could lose. Get and stay tuned in to what the competition is doing.
- Is what you offer truly seasonal? Is there a "best time"? If so, be there. You can try until the cows come home to even the mountains and valleys of sales, but a season is still a season. Don't miss it.

- Your traditional time is good, but maybe you can increase the action during your "slow time." Test. Make special offers—delay payments, offer premiums, test things to get the marginal buyer to become your customer now.
- Wave your mailings, spread your schedule, but not everything at once. Drop some over a longer schedule so you are visible over a continuing period of time.
- When are your customers buying? When do they want to buy? When is your product or service used the most, and how much lead time is necessary to hit that heavy-use season?

This last question is very important. If you sell boats, equipment, and supplies, the use season is usually several weeks to months after the buying season. If you sell fishing equipment by mail order, you may find your heavy season is several months before the fishing season begins.

Many businesses make buying decisions around the end of the month, the quarter, and the fiscal year for everything from pencils to heavy equipment to advertising services. Do you know the dates of your key customers' and prospects' fiscal year? If you sell to Hewlett Packard, you'll soon learn they work a November 1/October 31 fiscal year (it doesn't tie to anything—not the quarter, the calendar, nothing). If you sell to HP, you need to know this. You need to know it no matter who you sell to.

Schools in North America usually have a July/June year with 2 buying periods. Most U.S. federal government bodies work a July fiscal year with funding from October.

Financial planning and many similar factors are important as you decide the best time for you to be in the marketplace.

■ How to Set Direct Marketing Schedules ■

The second part of the timetable is the schedule itself. When and how should you plan to bring your product or service to the attention of your customer and prospect audience? What are the factors you need to consider as you set a schedule?

The forms, charts, and schedules that follow are work tools for you to adapt to your needs. They are guides at best, not a bible. Every company works differently and has different marketing objectives, goals, and budgets. The time frames on these charts are only IDEAS. They have all worked for me; they are an outgrowth of various programs I've worked on, which makes them neither right nor wrong—only IDEAS.

The Direct Marketing Schedule

This is a week-by-week timetable of how much time you should schedule to get various phases done (see Figure 3.2). A suggested length of time to complete each task in preparing a direct marketing program is listed.

Direct Mail

These tasks are for an "average" package, including a #10 or 6 × 9 outgoing envelope; a 1-, 2-, or 4-page letter; a business reply card and envelope; and a small brochure. It may be a 2- or 4-color package.

a. Research, copy, layout and design, including approvals and job cost estimate
b. Photography or creative art; final mechanical art for production
c. Market identification; list research, development, and ordering
d. Final production and lettershop services
e. Follow-up analysis and reporting, including recommendations

Direct Response Space Advertising

This includes either a black-and-white or color ad, with an 800 number and/or coupon.

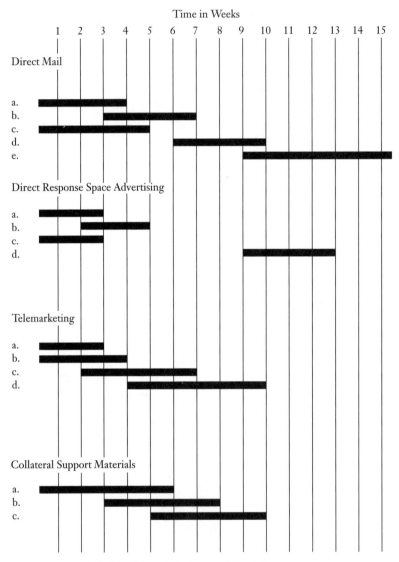

Figure 3.2 ▪ Weekly Direct Marketing Schedule

a. Research copy, layout and design, including approvals and job cost estimate
b. Photography or creative art; final mechanical art for production
c. Media plan, insertion schedule, and approvals
d. Follow-up analysis and reporting, including recommendations (depends on the insertion schedule; results can begin to be evaluated 1–4 weeks after the ad first appears)

Telemarketing

This includes all outbound calling programs.

a. Research and copy development, approvals, and job cost estimate
b. Market identification; list research, development, and ordering
c. Test calls and script testing (When telephone is used to complement a mail and/or space program, the start date for calling will vary with the program; however, 5 to 10 days after the prospect has received the printed message is usual.)
d. Follow-up analysis of test and reporting, including roll-out recommendations

Collateral Support Materials

Such materials include sales and sales promotion field-support brochures, flyers, fulfillment packages, premiums, and other marketing tools.

a. Research, copy, layout and design, including approvals and job cost estimate
b. Photography or creative art; final mechanical art for production
c. Final production

Basic Reverse Production Schedule

Many mailers use what is called a *reverse time schedule*. Here, you work backward. You look ahead to when you need to be in the marketplace and work back to the present, to where you are today. You then allocate your time accordingly. A typical reverse schedule might look like Figure 3.3.

Project title _____

Delivery date
to recipients _____   The date you want people to read and act on the mailing.

Mailing date _____   Allow extra time for the post office to deliver.

Assembly date _____   All components must be at mailer to ensure efficient operation.

Printing production
completion date _____   Allow time for inspection of lists before assembly.

Artwork approval
date _____   Artwork should be ready for the printer at this time.

Artwork completion
date _____   Allow time for as many approvals as necessary.

Finished artwork
starting date _____   Allow time for those inevitable interim changes.

Copy and layout
approval date _____   Allow enough time. If it isn't done right, everything suffers.

List order date _____   Check with your list broker to order far enough in advance.

Copy and layout
concept date _____   Everyone should be in agreement by this time.

Starting date _____   Allow think time for list research, planning, and testing.

Figure 3.3 ■ Sample Reverse Schedule

Direct Mail Lead Generation Planning and Schedule Chart

As with the other charts in this section, Figure 3.4 shows nothing more than one way to do something. It is offered as an example for you to use and adapt in planning your schedule. Because before you begin doing anything, you schedule everything!

Figure 3.4 was developed for a business mailer. The program was to be a 3-part direct mail lead generation effort. The 22 items listed and the 6-month time frame scheduled for this program are not "average" or "normal" or mandatory. This is simply what was planned. Katie Muldoon, a catalog expert, put together a similar schedule for a 48-page mail-order catalog. Her list included 54 tasks to be completed over a minimum of 26 weeks.

To make such a schedule, you need to know your company and the levels that must sign off on approvals, understand the sales force and its needs, and know the objectives of the campaign and the budget allowed. In this example, every area was touched. From the initial idea and concept stage, through all planning, program development, and organization, then the copy and art, the inbound and outbound telemarketing. Next came fulfillment, production, and lettershop. Last was follow-up and measurement. All steps were included—and scheduled.

Media Scheduling

Media scheduling is about frequency and impact. How often will you be in the marketplace and with what emphasis? There are countless media scheduling options. You dream it up and it can be done. There is certainly no "right" or "wrong" way.

Some of the things affecting what schedule you choose are the obvious factors of season and budget. If you're introducing a new product, your schedule will be different than if you're in a maintenance period.

	Week Starting	November					December		
		28	4	11	18	25	2	9	16
1.	Overall program direct mail series input	▬							
2.	General program concepts & development time		▬						
3.	Preliminary list research			▬▬▬					
4.	800 number/outbound phone & fulfillment services					●●●●●●●●●			
5.	General direction for creative—copy & art					═			
6.	Preliminary test grid structure					▬▬			
7.	Budget presentations and approvals						▬		
8.	Firm mailing lists & order for 3 mail drops							▬	
9.	Firm 800 number & fulfillment services								
10.	Present copy & art for first mailing							═	
11.	Begin development fulfillment package							═	
12.	Approval for first mailing								═
13.	Present copy & art for fulfillment								
14.	Approval for fulfillment package								
15.	Review program estimates								
16.	Final art approval for first mailing								
17.	Final art approval for fulfillment								
18.	Production for first mailing								
19.	Production for fulfillment package								
20.	Copy & art for second & third mail packages								
21.	Repeat creative & production for packages 2 & 3								
22.	DROP date for each of 3 mailings in series & program measurement								

Figure 3.4 ▪ Sample Lead Generation Planning and Schedule Chart

	January			Febuary				March				April	
23/30	13	20	27	3	10	17	24	3	10	17	24	31	7	14

Planning and program development, administration, budget and schedules, follow-up and measurement

Creative; all copy and art direction through final make-ready for production

800 number, telemarketing, fulfillment services, planning and coordination

Production process; all paper, printing, and lettershop services

✻   Mail dates for initial program

Here are 8 ways for you to schedule being in the marketplace (see Figure 3.5):

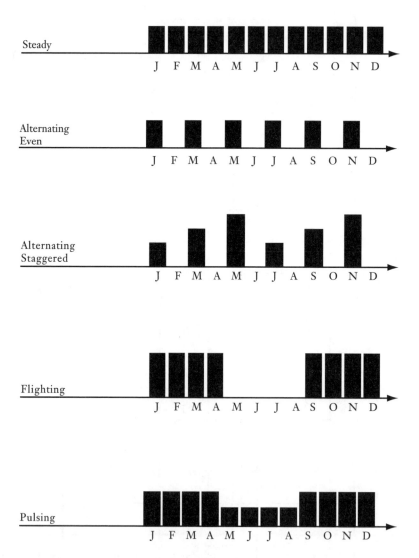

Figure 3.5 ■ 8 Ways to Schedule Media

Seasonal

J F M A M J J A S O N D

Teaser/
Step-Up

J F M A M J J A S O N D

Step-Down

J F M A M J J A S O N D

Figure 3.5 ■ (*continued*)

Steady

You are visible for an equal amount of time every month—a steady, continuing, and ongoing schedule. Very, very few marketers do this, except with corporate image campaigns.

Alternating Even

This is similar to the steady option, except you are visible every other month rather than 12 times a year. A few marketers do this, usually with print and broadcast efforts.

Alternating Staggered

This every-other-month effort builds up, drops back, and then builds again. This can be a good schedule when you have 2 very identifiable and seasonal selling seasons.

Flighting

You have a heavy program for a steady period, then nothing, then you get back in again. Many times, this is done on radio—usually for a very short period of time, such as 6 weeks in/6 out/6 in. It can also work in newspaper and even direct mail—in the marketplace every few weeks for several months, then out, followed by a repeat heavy schedule.

Pulsing

Pulsing is flighting on a continuing schedule—a heavy program, followed by a lighter one, and then a heavy one again. Print and broadcast are typical tools to use for pulsing campaigns. Sometimes the telephone is included to support the heavy time.

Seasonal

Just what it says, with this schedule you are in place only as your season approaches. This is very common with direct marketers who have a single, super heavy season.

Teaser/Step-Up

This is an accelerated seasonal effort, where you start small and peak at the height of your sales season. This also is a typical schedule for many in direct marketing, particularly those with consumer mail-order products.

Step-Down

The opposite of step-up. My feeling is that these 2 go together. Use step-up to lead to your heavy season, and keep the season going with a step-down schedule. It is a lesser campaign, but nevertheless a presence. First step-up, then step-down; working "two-gether."

There are really no "principles of scheduling." Direct mail is different than print and broadcast. Business-to-business schedules are different than those for consumers. Financial service products have a different timetable of promotion than consumables. Previous experience, common sense, and your budget will most often dictate your schedule.

▪ 9 Reasons You Need to Repeat Your Message ▪

It is a well-known fact that reach and frequency build awareness. Which generates interest. Which turns into a sale. Marketing has learned a couple of things from advertising. One of them is reach and frequency. Reaching your marketplace with a specific message and doing it on a repeated basis. Success is NOT a single effort! *Repetition builds your reputation.*

The Marketing Federation knows how important repetition is. Here are some of their ideas on repeating your message:

- Repeat for *reinforcement* or emphasis of a benefit or idea
- Repeat to aid in *understanding* any concept that may be difficult to understand
- Repeat if there is a possibility your message will not be *seen*
- Repeat when *expanding* on a key point
- Repeat for *"feeling"*
- Repeat for *credibility*
- Repeat for *dramatic impact*

The second thing marketing has learned from advertising is multimedia, where a number of different disciplines are used to repeat the message. My favorite example of a multimedia program, where the message was repeated over and over for several months, comes from the Bank of America. For a number of years, the bank made a major effort to increase its consumer loan base. The program was titled, "We've Got the Money." The bank used statement stuffers and direct mail to all its customers. It used outdoor posters, bus cards, radio, and television to noncustomers. It had a toll-free number for prospects to call for information, and developed an out-bound telemarketing program to follow all leads. It was a true multimedia effort, meshing the techniques of advertising and direct marketing for a most effective campaign.

Bank of America proved *repetition builds your reputation.* Let's look closely at 9 reasons WHY.

1. Your audience forgets 90% of what they see and hear within two weeks. Why is this so? Because there are hundreds of messages aimed at us every day. We are exposed to 570 advertising, public relations, sales promotion, and marketing messages a day. Of these, we "see" or "hear" only 80 and remember an even dozen—3 of which we recall negatively.

The results are the same in Adelaide, Bangkok, Caracas, Dakar, Edmonton, and Frankfurt—all around the globe the same thing happens. Every day. So, there is a strong need for you to repeat your message because of all the "noise" in the marketplace. Much is happening.

2. Your market changes constantly. My dad worked for the same company for 39 years. Thirty-nine years! Is there any chance you will work for the same company for half that time? Certainly not in today's marketplace.

Your market changes. Because we move. Because we have increasingly better communication and transportation. Because we get bored. Because we want new challenges, we want to dive into new opportunities. And when your market changes, you have to chase the new market. Which means you need to repeat your message.

3. You need to test new ideas on a continuing and ongoing basis. And retest the old ideas. In direct marketing you need to test new lists, new offers, new prices, new audiences, new geography, different media. Because your marketplace is like an octopus—it moves around a lot—you need to learn how best to reach it. And you need to do that on a continuing and ongoing basis. Ditto for old ideas you once used that worked, but that you no longer use. Try them again. Test, test, *test.*

4. You need to reach for new business. Early in my marketing and sales career, I lost two thirds of my business within 60 days. One of my major accounts went bankrupt. Another decided to walk. Because I had not been searching for new business, it took me 9 months to get even! Every week since, I spend a little time reaching for new business—talking to new people, looking into new marketplaces, trying to find where I might do my thing with another audience. You really do need to reach for new business.

5. You need to talk to your customers on a constant basis. Part of my time in this business was spent under the wing of Eric J. Smith, the Smith of Smith & Hemmings, a direct marketing agency. Eric taught me many things, one being the importance of staying in close and constant touch with your customers. He used to say, "Make love to your customers." Be their teddy bear, their security blanket. Hold their hand. Let them know you care.

Part of finding new business is talking to your current customers. They are probably your best source of additional new business. Talk to your marketplace. Make certain they know what you're up to. Most of us don't talk to our customers nearly as often as we should. We're afraid we may bother them. My recommendation is, bother them a little bit more. You'll probably get a little more business.

How often is too often? I don't know. I do know of a mail-order company in the United States that sends a direct mail package to a selection of its total marketplace 80-plus times in a single year! Is that too much? Not for those people. This company isn't mailing to keep the paper mills in business. It's mailing to be profitable. And it is. United Airlines, my choice for most of my business travel, "talks" to me more than twice a month. Between mail, e-mail, and the occasional telephone call, they stay in touch with their best customers.

You too need to talk with your customers more often.

6. You must constantly promote your offer. There is no reason for you to think I remember what your offer is, who you are to make it to me, or why I should respond to it. McGraw-Hill Research provides the graph shown in Figure 3.6, which shows how a full-page ad run in a business publication 13 times in 16 months continues to

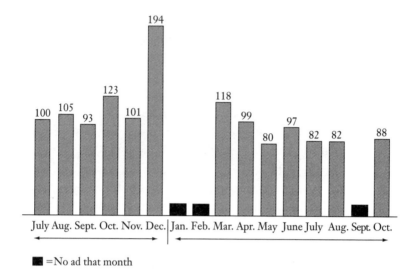

Figure 3.6 ■ Inquiries Generated from a Repeated Ad in a Monthly Publication

pull leads month after month. Five times during the campaign, the repeated insertions generated more inquiries than the initial ad.

You need to promote your offer on a continuing basis, using multimedia as necessary. Use a combination of mail, press, telephone, the World Wide Web, radio and/or television, trade shows, take-ones, and other disciplines and marketing tools. All to let your audience know what you offer and to make it easy for your prospects to contact you. Let them know how they can benefit by doing business with you. Make your offer desirable—and promote it.

7. You need to ASK FOR THE ORDER. McGraw-Hill learned it takes an average of 7 times for 1-on-1 sales representatives to ask for the order before they get it. Wow, 7 times! Sales & Marketing Executives International did a study with its membership. Its research showed that 81% of all sales are made on the fifth contact or later. Another WOW!

What this says is that you need to ask for the order over and over, again and again. You need to repeat your offer, repeat the benefits, repeat the request for action, and ask your prospects and customers to give you additional business.

AFTO—Ask for the Order!

8. You need continuity in the marketplace. You need to talk to your marketplace on a regular schedule. Not necessarily the same amount every week or every month, but on a regular basis. Do whatever makes the most sense, not just in and out at your convenience. You are more likely to be remembered when it's time to buy if you are seen frequently through the press, at a trade show, through a piece of direct mail, on radio or television, at your Web site— whatever is appropriate for your marketplace.

Yes, there are seasons, and sometimes a product can be sold only during that season. Valentine's Day products are sold in early February, St. Patrick's Day things during the middle of March. For most products and services, the seasons vary little. The range between the best and worst season is rarely more than 20%. This does not mean you shouldn't be aware of the differences. It does mean you need to be in the marketplace continually.

9. You need continuity of sales efforts. No matter how you sell—through a captive sales force, a telemarketing unit, a distribution network of some type, a retail store, the Web, or a combination of methods—you need to always have your sales force selling for you.

If you repeat your message to your marketplace on some sort of a regular schedule, your sales efforts will reflect the marketing. The sales team will find it easier to close sales because your presence in the marketplace is more active. Continuity in the marketplace and continuity of sales effort tie closely together.

Repetition builds your reputation—it really does! Jumping in and out of the marketplace on an infrequent basis, using only one media option, and making the same offer over and over is going to wear out. Soon, your marketplace will not "see" you. So, when you plan your marketing program, plan to be visible on a regular basis. Remember these 9 reasons for repeating your message the next time you do your marketing planning.

■ Typical Response Curve ■

Look at Figure 3.7. Is this typical—whatever that means? Well, yes and no. I include it to make a point. The point being you MUST be ready to handle the response to your program. In this example the activity is quick and sharp, lasting only a few weeks, falling off steadily over 6–7 weeks, and then dragging on for months. It is not a bell-shaped curve.

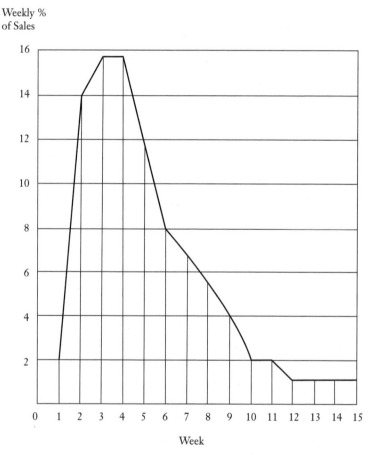

Figure 3.7 ■ Typical Response Curve

You need to be ready to provide your service during the initial peak as well as long afterward. Years ago, I was involved with a grand opening traffic-building program for a fast-food outlet. We mailed several thousand special coupon offers to households in the area. The program was outstandingly successful. In fact, it was too successful. There was so much traffic that by the middle of Saturday afternoon we were out of hot dog buns—a near disaster, if your product is hot dogs! (This particular problem was solved by rushing to the local supermarkets and buying every package of hot dog buns in sight.)

Another near crisis was a lead generation program for a high-tech company. The product was new, a true breakthrough in its field. It was introduced at trade shows, through direct mail and print advertisements in selected publications, and with postcard decks. It was a true multimedia program. A free information booklet was offered to generate leads. A toll-free number was available to those who couldn't wait for the mail. Outbound telemarketing was scheduled to follow up the fulfillment, to qualify the leads for the field sales force. The program was thoroughly organized. We expected to generate about 2,000 leads per month. All was set to handle this volume. What happened? Over the first 5 months of the campaign, 26,000 leads were generated—9,000 in a single month! It doesn't take much imagination to guess we were in trouble. We were not prepared for this avalanche and had to do some real dancing to catch up.

What is typical? There is no such thing. Just as *you* are not average, neither is any direct marketing program. You can't assume you'll get a certain response over a set time. It doesn't work that way. Sure, you can and should plan based on what happened last year. And if there wasn't a last year, use industry statistics.

When you use business magazines for lead generation, your replies will start slowly and build over a period of time. Longer than a similar direct mail program to the same audience with the same offer. Figure 3.8 is an example of what you might expect.

Sometimes your suppliers are a good source of knowledge about what your response might be. Talk to those people—the paper people, the envelope houses, the list brokers and lettershops, the magazine

Response

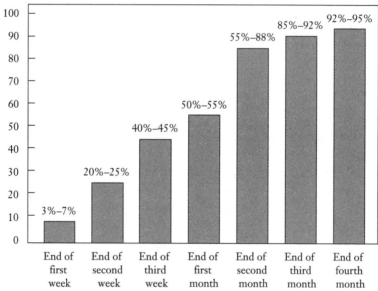

Figure 3.8 ▪ Accumulative Magazine Direct Response

reps, and the Web site builders. These people work daily with firms like yours and could be your best source of what is happening today.

When all else fails, your gut feeling may be as good as any other information you're going to get.

▪ MAILING/DISTRIBUTION PATTERN ▪

Figure 3.9 shows examples of how four types of mail-order catalogs were distributed by month. The business-to-business catalog had the largest range of distribution patterns throughout the year, with an extremely heavy drop in January and a quick falloff through the spring to the low point in June. Distribution picked up through the summer months to peak again in September, and then there was a quick falloff to the end of the year.

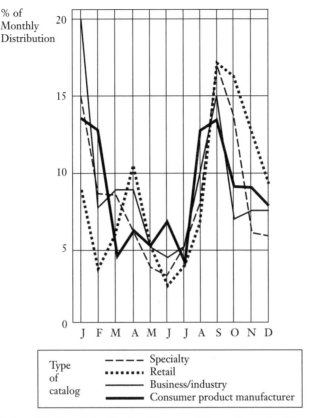

Figure 3.9 ▪ Mailing/Distribution Patterns Throughout the Year

The specialty catalog also had heavy January distribution, fell off through the spring, had a low point in June, and then quickly dropped to December.

The consumer products catalog had the most even distribution, even though high points in January and September mirrored the other catalogs. Its lowest distribution month was July.

The retail catalog really had 3 peaks. The first was a fairly heavy January, a little heavier second occurred in April, and the peak was in September. June was the low month for retail also.

What does all this say? As in all scheduling, you need to be in the marketplace when the buyer is ready to buy. Yes, many times you can "peak-the-peaks"; that is, get more out of the marketplace than your competition by being more aggressive and maybe a little earlier. But there are certain things you really cannot change. The May/June/July distribution patterns for all the catalogs are exceptionally low. Only unusual or special offers, new product introductions, and seasonal items will change that.

Even though these are "averages" from a survey by *Catalog Age*, you must still find the best time for *you*, whether it be by catalog or some other method. A quick glance at this chart may give you the misconception that the patterns between these 4 different styles of catalogs are alike. They are similar, but they are certainly not alike. In fact, there is a big difference between the business-to-business catalog and the retail catalog. The business catalog peaks in January and September. The retail catalog is good in January and peaks again in April and September. They're both low during June. Compare that with the consumer catalog, which peaks in January and September but has low points in March, May, and July. So, although there are similarities, there are also distinct differences. You must find the differences in scheduling to reach your marketplace. It *does* make a difference.

A. Eicoff & Company, a direct response agency specializing in broadcast, shares information on the best time for direct response television (see Figure 3.10). Wednesday is shown as the worst day of the entire week. The best day is Sunday. Prime time is not as productive as fringe time.

Richard Sangerman of Eicoff tells a story about one of the firm's clients, *Playboy*. Through some unusual circumstances, they tested a 1-minute subscription offer during the third quarter of a Chicago Bears football game. Two orders were received. Two! From a program directed toward one of the larger Chicago television audiences. Why only 2? Think about it: If you were a Bears fan, would you interrupt your Sunday afternoon enjoyment to order a magazine? If you leave the room to call the toll-free number you may miss an important play in the game. See that same offer at fringe time, when John Wayne is riding over the mountain to meet Big Chief (during a movie you've already seen 3 times), and you are much more likely to respond.

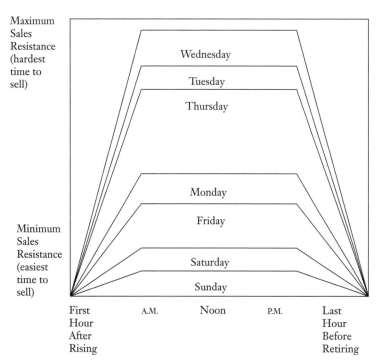

Figure 3.10 ■ The Best Time for Direct Response Television

Timing is important in every phase of direct response. Or, as good friend Bob Perlstein, president of Lifestyle Change Marketing, says, ". . . you must deliver the right offer to the right market at the right time. Timing can be everything."

The important part of any schedule is to have one! The second most important factor in scheduling is to include both everything possible and everyone necessary BEFORE actually starting a project. This will save you countless headaches, not to mention mistakes, budget misunderstandings, surprises, and schedule delays down the line. Plan ahead. Schedule early.

This is power direct marketing.

Chapter 4

BUDGET

Everything Costs More than You Think

■ ■ ■

I can't give you ball park figures, Al. The best I can do is Ball-parkish figures.

From the cartoon "Dollars and Nonsense"

Power direct marketing also includes that most painful area of every program—the budget. Money. The cost of doing what we desire, want, and need to do to reach our objectives.

Advertising, public relations, and, YES, direct marketing are an investment, not an accounting function and NOT an expense! Marketing should be treated as an opportunity to expand your horizons, to grow, to conquer, to do things that generate the most revenue for the least amount of cash.

Far too often, we "wing" it. We use the SWAG method of setting a budget (Scientific, Wild, Aspiring Guess) Not good! To help avoid the SWAG method, budget is the third point of The 8ight Point Plan.

▪ Some Questions to Consider ▪

Here are some things to consider as you plan the budget for your direct marketing program:

1. What is your definition of a budget? What do you include under the heading of budget? Not everyone agrees in this area. You must include everything and every item you feel fits.
2. What is your budget history for this product or product line? Where have you invested your advertising and marketing dollars in the last year? In the last 2 years?
3. Can you make your budget flexible to take advantage of an opportunity? When you know the value of a customer, can you set your budget based on how many new customers you can get at an acceptable cost?
4. Where do you see the major emphasis for your budget for the coming year? Is that different than in the recent past?
5. What is your prime competitor's share of the market? How does it compare to yours? How much do they invest to maintain their share? Where do they spend it—in what media?
6. Monthly/quarterly/annually, what is your total advertising and marketing budget for this product line? Will it be available on an accelerated schedule, if necessary, to meet seasonal opportunities? What about a special or an unusual situation?

The Business Marketing Association has cranked out a series of white papers over the years, including one on budgeting. It suggests 4 primary areas of difficulty with setting budgets and making them work:

▪ The person charged with the power to approve marketing budgets lacks understanding of what marketing is and does.

- Budgets seem to be the first item cut when business conditions change—whether or not they are in line and performing according to plan.
- There is a lack of willingness or ability to measure budgets against objectives, which is mandatory in direct response to set future realistic budgets.
- It is difficult to forecast accurately the amount of funding needed to really reach specific objectives.

When a campaign is approved, the budget becomes an integral part of the plan, just as important as the other elements of the plan. It is equal to the objectives, the timetable, the message carried in the copy and art, the media. The budget should be changed ONLY when the plan itself is changed.

▪ HOW TO BUDGET FOR DIRECT RESPONSE PROGRAMS ▪

Let's begin with some ways *not* to set your direct marketing budget. How often have you heard (or used) the following explanations?

- "We spent what was spent last year. If we did anything else I'd have to explain it."
- "We matched the competition."
- "We relied on the agency's suggestions."
- "We separated all the parts, assigned a figure, and added it up."

In direct response, the product or service category hardly matters in setting a sound budget. Budgets that work are those based on your objectives and timetable. Those that are less likely to work are thrown together using the SWAG approach. Beginning with specific objectives for your direct marketing program—knowing the numbers you aim to achieve—will make setting the budget just that much easier. And it is more likely to be on target because your objectives are numeric.

How much should you invest? I don't know. How should you determine what to invest? By answering these questions:

- What is your product? Is it a business or consumer product?
- What response can you expect to your best offer?
- What dollar value can you expect from your average order?
- What is the competition doing?
- What is your markup? The spread you have to work with?
- What will the marketplace accept?
- Is your product a new product introduction, a standard in the industry, a commodity, or a mature product?
- Where are you in the marketing cycle of this product line?
- What additional offers can you make to your customer base after acquisition?

Okay, how much *should* you invest? It all depends. It depends on many factors. For example, food service works on small margins and high volume. Luxury items have more money to play with.

In direct marketing budgeting, the elements to be concerned with are as follows:

- The cost of reaching your audience, meaning the total dollars invested and the cost per thousand
- The response generated from your audience, meaning the total number of responses and the number of responses per thousand
- The promotional cost per response, meaning the cost per lead or inquiry and the cost per order or sale

Most business-to-business manufacturers budget somewhere in the 2%–5% of sales range, those in mail order from 20%–30% of sales. I have worked on projects where we spent less than 1% of projected sales; others went over 50%. It all depends.

What should you include in your budget? Everything that fits! All promotional costs, including:

- Trade shows
- Print advertising
- Public relations for the program
- Direct mail
- Telemarketing
- A toll-free number
- A Web site
- Sales support and fulfillment materials
- Point-of-purchase displays
- Premiums and advertising specialties
- Postcard decks
- Radio and/or television

Put in anything and everything you plan to include as part of this direct response effort.

What should you NOT include? I recommend all sales, sales staff, and sales service costs—mostly people and related expenses— NOT be included in your direct marketing budgets. They need their own budgets, their own controls. In most cases, you'll have no difficulty separating sales from marketing. Sales management will recognize, as you do, that you are talking about 2 different disciplines. Marketing is an activity that directs the flow of your business. Salespeople work that activity and gain a close, get the order. They belong in different budget categories. Don't mix them; you'll both regret it.

▪ 3 STYLES OF BUDGETING ▪

There are 3 specific ways or methods for you to consider as you establish a budget.

The Sales Turnover Approach

It is traditional to take a flat percentage of sales and appropriate this sum as the budget. This is common when the product is established and the market is clearly identifiable. Usually the amount is fixed against the previous year's actual sales. Sometimes it will be based on projections for the coming year. Many consumer marketers use this approach; it is used less frequently in the business-to-business field.

The Share of Marketing Expense Method

In many large organizations, each share or individual part of the total program is isolated and a marketing communications budget is set for that specific tool. You look at all of the planned activities, including direct marketing, general advertising, sales promotion, public relations, and all their pieces, and allocate a fixed budget for each according to how you see that function working as part of the whole. You then divide the total pie by what you believe to be the best mix to bring you the maximum results for your investment.

This is a very subjective approach, with a lot of feeling and emotion entering into the process. This is not to say it is not a valid method of budget setting—it is. Companies that assign a large dollar amount to marketing and advertising activities many times find this a good way of agreeing on their budget.

The Task Method

Under the task method, you assign a money amount to what you feel is necessary to achieve your specific objectives. You look first at projected results, not costs. You look at your goals, you evaluate the marketing tools and expenses you deem necessary to achieve those goals, and from that planning effort you create a budget. You establish a budget to accomplish a task.

This is very common among direct marketers. Many direct marketing projects are just that—projects—thus, only the task method is truly workable. This method is also popular with industrial firms. It applies equally well whether the new products or services being launched are business or consumer.

A Task Method Example

Because the task method is so popular in direct marketing, here's an example of how it works.

Let's create a sales situation. You are an organization with an outside field sales force. You sell business-to-business. The sales team works off leads to make appointments to give a demonstration that leads to a sale.

You have determined that each member of your sales staff of 5 needs 3 fresh leads each week. A total of 15. Figuring a 45-week year, that is a grand total of 675 leads (5 staff × 3 leads × 45 weeks = 675).

You have a fairly high-ticket item and can invest up to $100 to generate the lead. This means your marketing budget for the year can be set at $67,500 (675 leads × $100 = $67,500).

Up to this point, it is fairly straightforward and simple because we "assumed" a few things. We assumed you'll get 675 *qualified* leads, each ready for a sales visit and demo. Highly unlikely!

We have not said anything about closing ratios. Even with 675 qualified leads, how many will the sales force close? What is the ratio—1 of 3, 2 of 5?

We also haven't talked about the potential audience. How large is it? If it is 15,000 or 150,000, how do you approach the market?

What we really haven't asked in this example is *how much are you willing to invest for a sale?* Cost per sale is the all-important number. Cost per lead is nice to know, still, it doesn't get the order.

Let's go back now, fill in some of the blanks, and see where that takes us, how it helps. First, the close ratio. History tells us your experienced sales force will close 1 of every 2 qualified leads. Based on experience from the last 2 years, for every 3 leads generated, 1 was worthy of a personal follow-up sales call. One of 3 was qualified to receive a presentation. If you close 1 of 2, that means you can invest up to $200 in marketing expenses to get a sale. (If you could afford $100 for the lead and you were happy with the 1 in 2 close, that must mean you're happy with the $200 figure.)

Further, if it takes 3 leads to get 1 demo and you want to hold to a total of 675 presentations for the year, that means you need to generate 2,025 leads (which yields 675 qualified leads, 1 of 3).

All of which says you can invest $33.33 to produce a lead ($67,500 ÷ 2,025 total leads = $33.33). This certainly makes the program look different than when we looked at it with a $100 per lead cost.

You can now decide, from the available audience, where you want to put your efforts. Is it possible to select from the total those most likely to buy now? What about those you talked to last year who didn't buy but could have? Should you chase them this year?

We also know you have "only" $33.33 to generate a lead, not $100. That's a big difference, an important difference, up front. If you were not planning your budget against your objectives, you just might overlook it.

In this example, we had a specific task to get 675 qualified leads for your sales force. By setting a budget with specific numbers in mind, you can create a better direct marketing program. You are more attuned to the audience selection, offer, creative, and media options open to you. Your program becomes better and enjoys a much higher probability of success.

∎ Allowing Enough Money and Time ∎

Marketing expenses stimulate growth. Their overall objective is to earn you a return in the form of more profits. The budget should not be a cost item; it should be an investment in your company and its growth and profits.

Marketing also should be appreciated for its long-term value. Far too many times I've heard the statement, "We tried direct mail once." Or, "Yes, we tried a telemarketing program. It didn't work."

Or similar. So what? It is a rare occasion when you are successful the first time you try something. There is a reason we have erasers on pencils. Sometimes it doesn't work the way we want it to work the first time. Or the second. As with all programs that are "art," there is lots of room for opinion. That is one of the blessings of direct response marketing. It allows for many options. There are many ways to get from where you are to where you want to go.

"Test, test, test" is direct marketing's middle name. So, in addition to taking the time it may take to be successful, you also need to budget to be successful. Thinking ahead, it is also best to allow for "new" things in your budget as opportunities appear.

A marketing campaign works best when it is maintained, when it gets a steady push over time. You don't want starts and stops—aim for starts and slowdowns, followed by speed-ups; that is, a continuing program. Can you name 3 prime-time television commercials that you know ran only one time? What about outdoor posters or bus cards—are they in only one location? And magazine or newspaper corporate ads—are they placed in one publication one time only? Sometimes, but rarely. Why? Because your reputation improves with repetition. The more your prospective audience sees and hears from you, the more likely they are to become your good customers.

When you budget, you must think ahead, not just for the immediate program, but beyond. To do otherwise is to be counterproductive. Thinking and planning ahead includes your direct marketing budget.

Budgets are usually conceived for a year at a time. In direct response, they sometimes cover a shorter time (quarterly is not uncommon) or a single project. None of these methods are all good or all bad. They are different. Shorter and smaller may be best. Particularly with small companies, a new product launch, or an expansion. Any time it might be better to have more flexibility so you can respond quickly to a market opportunity.

As with everything else in marketing, planning and commitment are keys to success. A commitment to a direct response program is also a commitment to the budget to implement that program. They come as a package. Which is why budget is an important step in The 8ight Point Market Action Plan.

▪ TOGETHERNESS ▪

The first 3 points of The 8ight Point Plan must fit together. Why? Because sound objectives, to be achieved within a reasonable time frame with sufficient budget, make for a good program. Any variation on that theme will bring less than optimal results. If your objectives are designed to fit the marketplace, but either the time allotted to accomplish them or the budget allocated does not mesh, the program will fail.

Many times, we set high objectives. Fine, as long as you assign both time and money to reach those high goals. If you do not, then something has to give. You may need to alter the time assigned or the budget, or even lower your expectations. Possibly some of each.

Rarely do we wish to reduce our goals. Yet my experience has shown over and over that when sufficient time and adequate budget are not available, your objectives will not be reached. Someone will say, "We tried that once. It didn't work." Don't do that to yourself! As you plan your program, include in your planning the knowledge that all the pieces go together to make the whole. Shortchanging yourself anywhere along the line will hurt.

It doesn't matter nearly as much *what* your objectives, your schedule, and your budget are, as it does that they *exist*. Make sure they work together, complement one another. Plan it!

Power direct marketing begins with the first 3 points of The 8ight Point Market Action Plan (Objectives, Timetable, and Budget), which must fit together like hand in glove. Like the pieces of a puzzle—snug, tight, and comfortable.

Chapter 5

AUDIENCE

TARGET MARKETING IS LIKE DIVING 75 FEET INTO A BUCKET OF WATER

■ ■ ■

What our business is is NOT determined by the producer, but by the consumer!

Peter Drucker

Now that you have stated your objectives, a workable timetable, and a budget, you're ready to fire away. Yet, remember the sequence: Ready, Aim, Fire! Aiming at your audience is crucial to your success. Audience is the fourth point in The 8ight Point Market Action Plan.

Your single most important asset is your audience, your core marketplace. If you haven't clearly identified your market, you have very little chance of reaching it. Your audience is the key element in any marketing package. Without proper identification of the audience, the offer and creative development go for naught.

■ Some Questions to Consider ■

1. What is the size of the market for your product line? How can that market be expanded? Exploited?
2. Is your product to be marketed to particular segments of the community? Can you clearly identify those segments?
3. Has research defined the measurable characteristics of the prospective customer?
4. Who are your current customers? What do you know about them? Can you overlay any common characteristics? How many customers do you have?
5. Does the profile of your current customer meet the profile of your potential customer? If not, what is the profile of your best prospects?
6. What do the current customers buy in products and services? How long do they remain customers? What additional products and services can be sold to them?
7. What do your customers think your strengths and weaknesses are? What *are* your strengths and weaknesses?
8. Who are your competitors? What do your customers think about them?
9. How long has it been since you've talked to your sales staff about your customers?
10. How long has it been since you talked face-to-face with several of your customers?

In direct mail and telemarketing, your audience is your list. In direct response space advertising and on the Web, your audience is your readership. In radio, it is your listeners; in television, your viewers.

You may have a situation where your direct mail or telephone list is a captive group, very vertical. It may include only your own customers or clients. Even in these instances, many times the customers don't know why you're coming to them at this time. And they won't know until you talk to them and make them an offer. In communication with your own customers, it is important to always remember they are your most important asset. Treat them well.

The audience is equally important if you have a cold list, one with customers who have no prior relationship with you, your company, or your products or services. Whether you are looking for leads from business or consumer prospects, reaching into the market to develop a traffic-building program for a retail outlet, conducting a business or consumer mail-order sales effort, or endeavoring to raise funds for a community/school/charity project, in every instance you must massage, court, woo, measure, and account for those prospects. They are your audience for this particular offer.

■ TARGET MARKETING VERSUS MASS MARKETING ■

Years ago Ed Mayer, the dean of education for the direct mail industry, devised a formula that went like this: 40% of the success of your direct response program is selecting the right list; 40% is making the best possible offer to this highly selected audience; and 20% is the creative, the copy, and the art. Today, the concept is the same, but *the numbers have changed dramatically.* They look like this:

Category	Target Marketing	Mass Marketing
Audience	60%	20%
Offer	30%	40%
Creative	10%	40%

Let's begin with the mass marketing approach. With prime-time television, a general news magazine, a daily newspaper, or a similar medium, the audience reach is broad. Thousands, hundreds of thousands, and even millions of people are reached with a "general" message to buy Pepsi or a specific Kellogg's cereal. Or maybe a more select product, a high-ticket item such as a Lincoln Continental. A mass appeal also might be made for a personal computer from Dell or Gateway.

At any given time the audience selection is poor at best; only a very few of us are in the marketplace for any of these products at any one time. The audience reach is truly to the masses, playing the numbers game, hoping to get enough of the right people at the right time.

The offer is important in mass marketing. Price is one of the key advertising offers. Competition is keen for soft drinks, breakfast foods, automobiles, and discretionary income that could certainly apply to whether or not we decide to purchase a home computer. A good offer is made to get us to consider a particular product now.

And creative is obviously key to getting the attention of those few people from the masses who might be ready at this particular moment to make a buying decision. Which is why so much is invested in preparing outstanding creative print or outdoor ads or television commercials—to get our attention.

Target marketing is entirely different. Direct response allows you to identify your market, reach it, and talk with it. Your message is aimed at a particular audience. The tighter you can be with your audience, the more likely you'll turn up a winner.

Juergen Aumueller, former president of American Express Travel Related Services, Germany, said:

> The similarities between AmEx cardholders around the world far outweigh the differences. They display a vast range of tastes but are remarkably similar in all of the markets in which we operate. These insights led us to challenge the orthodox view that local is best.
>
> We have repositioned our product, our communications, indeed our organization, within a global context . . . personal service reigns supreme, mandating the strategic use of a personalized medium such as direct mail.

Mr. Aumueller was targeting the AmEx market. If your creative is outstanding but you direct it to the wrong audience, you will fail. If your offer is sound, solid, competitive, fitting for the marketplace, and aimed at the wrong audience, you will fail.

Please, please, please do NOT send me anything about gardening. Yes, I live on a ranch in an area surrounded by fields of lettuce, carrots, watermelons, and many other crops. I still do not garden. I will not mow my nearly 3 acres of grass, trim the hedges or countless trees, rake the leaves, prune the roses, weed, water, fertilize, or perform any other activity related to gardening. I don't do those things! And, no matter your offer or the quality of your creative approach, I am still not a prospect for any product or service even remotely tied to gardening. I am clearly the wrong audience.

The creative process is very important. Carefully considering and then selecting the right offer is vital to the success of your direct response program. In fact, both these subjects are so important they each have their own point as part of The 8ight Point Market Action Plan ("Offer" is covered in Chapter 6, "Creative" in Chapter 7). Yet separately, and even collectively, they are not as important as selecting the right audience.

In target marketing, the audience is the key element, clearly number one in importance to the success of your total direct marketing program.

▪ WHY CAREFUL AUDIENCE SELECTION IS VITAL ▪

Freewheeling advertising spending is being replaced by smart, careful target market spending. Image advertising is being replaced by product-specific marketing campaigns. General advertising media are being replaced by target market tools that zero in on your best audience and talk to them with a specific message of interest. These programs are each designed to gain a lead for a sales force, to build traffic at a consumer or business retail store, or to make a sale by mail order. They involve products and services used either at the office or in the home.

The last 2 decades of the 20th century introduced more media vehicles than were ever dreamed of prior to the electronic age. Today, we are in the age of overchoice, and still more media options have and are being developed, tried, and tested. Some will be successful; some will not. We're all affected by these new ways to reach our customers and prospects, to identify and reach our best audiences. The end result is a much more fragmented, segmented, targeted marketplace to reach into, to select from, and to sell to. Niches are everywhere.

Direct marketing as a technique to reach a target market has grown dramatically since World War II. Why? Well, for one reason, the primary mission of any marketing program is to be *both* effective and efficient. BOTH! Something direct marketing is good at, provided the right audience selection happens at the start. Unfortunately, it is possible to be effective and cost-inefficient. It is also possible to be efficient with monies and totally off the mark with effectiveness.

Cost efficiency is relative. Against your goals and objectives you must consider the product, the offer, and—the key ingredient in all communication—the audience. Cost per impression of contact is not really all that important. Cost per lead is somewhat important and is certainly both interesting and helpful in future planning. *Cost per SALE* is the important factor! It doesn't matter what it costs to make a contact or gain a lead. It doesn't matter what the cost is to qualify that prospect or handle fulfillment. It matters considerably what it costs to sell that prospect, to turn the prospect into a customer, to make the sale, to get the order.

Getting the sale efficiently and effectively will turn a profit for your company, which is really what the entire marketing process is all about. And you can be both effective and efficient only when you begin your direct marketing efforts with accuracy in audience identification. Remember, the message must be right for the audience. More importantly, the audience must be right for the message. You must take accurate aim to hit your target.

■ The Importance of Keeping Customers ■

A good name is better than precious ointment.

Ecclesiastes 7:1

The most important asset of any business is its list of customers. Your customer base depreciates faster than any machine or building and is more valuable than all your buildings and equipment.

Your business customer base is subject to attrition for a number of reasons. Death is one; companies go away. They fail, they fold, they merge, they move, they divide—and you no longer have a customer. In most instances, there is little you can do about it. Ditto for your consumer customer base. The move rate in the United States has remained fairly constant at around 20% annually for a number of years. Younger folks move more often, so do those who live in apartments. With job promotions, 2 income households, smaller families, later marriages, and longer life spans, the consumer customer is also changing.

Customers also go away because your good competition takes them from you. Your competitors offer something you do not—a true benefit your customer feels is over and above what you offer. It could be something as simple as convenience or location. They just plain have something better, and your customers like it. They move on.

Customers also go away because of indifference shown by YOU! You, your company, and all your people. You fail to express the interest, the caring, the understanding that customers need. You are not in step with your customers, so they elect to march with a different band.

A customer costs little to maintain with regular contacts. The costs of keeping a customer are far less than the costs of obtaining a new one. Some experts have said maintenance and service are only 10% of the cost of new business acquisitions.

Your best source of new business is your current customers! They already know you. You have built a trust, provided a service or product. Finance, operations, manufacturing, administration, sales, and customer service—all elements in providing for a customer—are in place, already doing the job.

Gaining more business from your current customers is easy compared with going into the marketplace and starting from scratch. If you have a new product, try it first on your customers. A new service, another plant or office, expanded staff, other enhancements or upgrades, improvements, something truly new or different—whatever it is, your customers are more likely than anyone else to say YES to your presentation and offer.

So, the best audience for your business is that group already doing business with you—your customers. Chase them, ask them to give you more of their business. Surprisingly enough, if you ask, you will receive—especially from those who are already comfortable doing business with you.

■ Profile of Your Audience: A Portrait of 1 ■

I would to God thou and I knew where a commodity of good names were to be bought.

Shakespeare, *King Henry IV*

Selection of the right audience is the single most important element in every direct response marketing program. Without proper identification of the audience, your offer, all creative development, and everything else is for nothing.

How much can you afford to spend to get a new customer? How much is that new customer worth to you over time? And, once you determine the answers to these 2 key questions, how do you find the right audience?

You begin by profiling your current customers. You clearly identify to whom you presently sell. If you are new or your product is new, your experience in the marketplace will help. Sometimes good, sound common sense works wonders. Asking others in the same or a similar field can give you direction. Surveys, in-depth research, or most likely a combination of several of these sources will provide you with a guide.

Ira Belth, a noted authority on business-to-business direct mail lists said a most interesting thing:

When it comes to direct response marketing you must appreciate a mailing list is NOT a mailing list. It is an alignment of carefully selected people—people to whom you want to sell something. To achieve a high effectiveness quotient, your campaign has to be delivered to the individual buyers, specifiers, and influencers.

The emphasis is on the *individual*. Because you must remember your collective audience is not a collection at all, it is one person at a time. No matter what you sell, its purpose or service, its price or value, its application for work or home, luxury or necessity, *people* make buying decisions. Your audience is a list of individuals.

You must know that the ideal audience for your product or services does exist somewhere. Standard Rate & Data Services (SRDS) may list it in one of their directories. A list broker may have it on file. It could be in the Yellow Pages or come from a trade industry or association membership list. It might be a special-interest magazine subscription file, or members of a church in your hometown, all students in the sixth grade, or women over the age of 40. It could be the 79 sugar beet processors in the United States or the 800 marble bathtub manufacturers. What about the 1,427 cotton ginners, 1,974 acupuncturists, 248 dude ranches, 5,258 logging camps, 327 beekeepers, 503 tattoo services, or 829 xylophone players.

The population in North America (Canada, Mexico, and the United States) exceeds 400 million. Collectively, there are about 20 million companies and over 155 million households within those 3 countries. There are clearly identifiable and reachable groups of chemical engineers, surgeons, optometrists, black opinion leaders, chief financial officers of Fortune 1,000 companies, meatpacking plants, school bus manufacturers, diaper services, and music libraries.

There are at least 40,000 different business lists, 30,000 mail-order buyer lists, and probably something close to 100,000 consumer mailing lists. Certainly a wide selection of sources for you to use in finding your right audience.

▪ The Value of Profiling ▪

You need to profile your audience and, from all available sources, find the right audience for you. The purpose of profiling is 2-fold: to determine what you can invest in getting a new customer; and to determine where these new prospects are most likely to be found.

If you have a customer base, the first thing you need to do is clearly and cleanly identify the common denominators in that audience:

- Job titles if it's a business list, or the group of titles that fits best
- Number of employees in those companies
- Standard Industrial Classification (SIC) code of the customer base
- Use of your product (its applications)
- Financial strength and rating

If your audience is consumers, identify what you know about that group of individuals:

- Age
- Sex
- Zip/postal code demographics
- Family size
- Marital status
- Length of time at the same address
- Hobbies and other interests
- Home value

Consumer and business marketers each want to know how many times prospects have bought and how frequently. Have they purchased by mail? What have they bought from others that relates to your product and service? How did they become your customers? What was the source of the business?

Identifying markets is not always easy; with direct marketing it can be complicated, even complex. And, it is so critical! Because, without the correct audience, it is highly unlikely you will be successful, even if the rest of your program is in place and ready to go. Even if it is implemented flawlessly.

When your penetration level of a particular segment gives you a high response, you can safely assume this identifies a niche with a high propensity to buy your product or service. On the other hand, if your penetration is low, it certainly does not mean this audience won't buy from you. It could mean any number of things. It could mean your offer wasn't targeted accurately. It could be your timing was off, the season was wrong. It could even be that you never asked for the order.

You will find your audiences in 3 main areas. They will come from your house lists, your response lists, and your compiled lists. They are from inside your building, your office, your company, your own files.

Business at Your Fingertips: House Lists

Long-time business friend and excellent direct marketer Doug Kercher and I have worked together for decades. From the programs we've shared come these thoughts about how you can improve your list selection from your house list.

House lists are made up from sales records, call reports, and general correspondence. Purchase orders carry valuable list-building information such as full company names, addresses and postal codes, those who have approved purchases, and to whom the material has been shipped.

If your sales reps make call reports, it's well to include space for mailing information on their report forms. Ask for basic data such as names to mail to, full addresses, types of material to be sent, phone and fax numbers, and e-mail addresses.

A regular check of correspondence through key departments in your company will most likely reveal additional names for your mailing list.

If you are a manufacturer, don't overlook your distributors' mailing lists. Getting them may be difficult, but if you plan ahead, it's often possible to include access to the mailing list as part of a contract with a new distributor. Distributors are often more than willing to have you mail to their prospects, because your promotion will benefit them. If nothing else works, you might even pay them for the use of their lists.

Advertising inquiries is another effective way to add to your house list. Responses to your advertising will provide good names. It's advisable to build some type of qualification system into your advertising program. For instance, you can offer a specific piece of literature that will be of interest only to key companies or specific titles. Call or write to a responsible company officer and say you are going to send literature. Ask for the name of the proper individual to whom it should go. You will be surprised at the excellent response you receive.

Trade show registration lists can be a very effective source for your house list. Trade shows can be used to develop names for your list, provided you qualify the prospects right on the spot and ask for names of others to whom your material should be sent. Among the usual methods of name collecting at trade shows are prize drawings, visitor guest logs, and literature request forms. Two of the more imaginative methods that have been used effectively are:

- **The use of a tape recorder.** The visitor picks up the microphone and gives his or her name, position, address, and the type of information wanted.
- **A "literature supermarket."** The supermarket is composed of a literature display, with a hook below each piece holding numbered tags. The visitor takes tags representing each piece of literature desired and attaches them to a business card or an address slip. Fulfillment is done following the show.

Now, a few points on the care and feeding of your house mailing list:

1. Plan your list; take time to look at future potential. Should you code by product, dollar value of purchases, date of purchase? By building in all considerations at the initial stage, you will be prepared for any future selectivity that may be required.
2. Make at least one first-class mailing to the list each year. The post office will return all undeliverable mail, so you can clean the list.
3. Keep a rough count of the additions, changes, and deletions made to the list in the course of a year. If these changes don't amount to at least 20% of the total, your list is probably decaying.
4. Add your name and home address (and those of several of your marketing team members) to the list. It will give you an idea of the timing of mailings.
5. Add a "dummy" or "seed" name to the list. It could be an incorrect spelling of your name. It will tell you quickly if your list is being used for some unauthorized purpose.

Interested Prospects: Response Lists

Response lists are the second major category. Response lists include those people who have responded to your marketing/advertising/ public relations program or to someone else's. This group has expressed some interest in your product or service or one that is similar or compatible to yours. You know something about these people. They are willing to be "found." They want information and are interested in making a buying decision. They bought by mail order or did something that lets you know they are prime prospects. These people have done something to be identified as interested in what you are offering:

- They clipped a coupon.
- They called a toll-free number.

- They mailed back a business reply card.
- They sent in a questionnaire.
- They walked into your store with your mailer or ad in their hand.
- They sent a fax.
- They responded to your Web site by e-mail.

Any one of these actions indicates they've seen and read something from you—your newspaper or magazine ad, your direct mail piece, something. And they responded, they took action.

The best prospects from the response lists are those who, in addition to expressing interest and asking for more information, did take the next step. They placed an order. By this positive move, they told you they were responsive, maybe mail-order responsive, but certainly responsive. They said they could be motivated by receiving a direct response message. If you can talk with the people who are interested in what you are offering—be it through your field sales force, through a network of dealers or distributors, by telemarketing, by mail-order catalog, with a demonstration, or via your Web site—you are likely to gain a sale. Response lists are more likely to gain you interested people to talk to and sell.

How do you choose response lists, and what is important about your selection of the right ones? Here are four key points in response list selection:

1. The people listed bought a product similar to yours from a competitor.
2. The product or service was priced close to yours.
3. They made a recent buying decision in a category close to yours.
4. They paid for it the same way you like to be paid.

These factors are especially important if you sell to consumers, but the same ideas are applicable to business, too. If possible, it would be nice to know the answers to each of these questions before you select the audience you are going to test.

Where do you find response lists? Here is a partial list of possibilities:

- Mail-order buyers
- Inquiry lists
- Subscription lists
- Bingo card responses
- Lead generation programs (using direct mail, print, broadcast, the Web, public relations, trade show registrations)
- Sweepstakes and contest entries

The Building Source: Compiled Lists

The fabric of society is forever changing, more so today than ever before. Experience shows most business lists change at a rate of 25%–35% annually. (My own very informal and totally nonscientific survey of marketing people shows this group churns even faster at 40%–70% each year.) Thus, no mailing list is ever perfect. Like the telephone book, it's wrong the day it comes off the press.

However, compiled lists offer you opportunities to reach your select audience, possibly better than any other source. Why? Well, compiled lists are built lists. You build them or someone else builds them. They come from scores of sources, and depending on your needs, your product, and your offer, they may be just right for you.

The compiled list category is the largest of the 3 we've discussed because you can build names from just about any source. It has been estimated that some lists in America total 500 billion people. Obviously, many lists include the same people many times over. Here are a few of the many sources for compiled lists:

- Government information
- Directory publishers
- Telephone company data
- Credit reports
- Trade associations

- Annual reports
- Almost any company where information is collected

From compiled lists, you know only what you know about the source and not much more. If they were compiled from an association directory of members of a specific organization, you know that and whatever characteristics are available on that group. Nothing else. If they were compiled from automobile registrations, you know the type, make, model, year of their cars with whatever additional "feelings" that tells you. And not much more.

You can, and probably should, overlay demographic data available from census information to expand your knowledge level about any particular prospect list and improve its worth to you. Psychographic data are obtainable from a few consumer lists by doing careful selection within specific categories and then matching. This, too, is something you should do if the option is open to you.

Overlays with business lists are a little tougher. You usually get name, title, company, division, mailing address, and telephone number. Less often, but still available, you find direct-dial fax numbers and e-mail addresses. Many times you can add the SIC code, which allows you to greatly increase your knowledge base. Within some lists, you can then obtain company-specific data piece by piece.

Many business and professional publications make their subscriber lists available. They can be an excellent list source. These lists are cleaned regularly by the publication mailing and other direct mail usage. They also provide the opportunity to complement advertising programs with select direct mail.

When evaluating lists for possible use, consider these points:

1. How often is the list updated?
2. What are the sources of names on the list? Are they customers or buyers? Do they subscribe to a magazine? Is the list personalized by name and title? Are the names those of companies only, drawn from a source such as the Yellow Pages?

3. How often is the list used? Does the list owner make regular mailings to the list (for example, a magazine or promotional mailings to buyers)?

4. Is there any "independent" means of ensuring the list quality? Business publication lists are subject to audit. This means names of qualified readers must be verifiable. Is this possible with the list you want to use?

5. What selections are available? Are there psychographic, demographic, and/or geographic selections?

6. Is the list in postal code order so you can benefit from reduced postal rates?

7. Can you get a sample of the mailing label or dump of the magnetic tape?

8. Because of their immense value to their owners, most lists are made available for one-time rental only. Some compiled lists are sold outright or for multiple use over a set time. How is this list available?

9. What type of company or organization uses the list? A good list owner will usually not disclose the names of other clients, but will let you know the types of businesses that have used it.

10. Is there a protected mailing date? In other words, will x number of other mailings be done to the same list the same week your mailing is sent?

11. Are the list counts accurate?

12. Keep records of cutoff points on list tests. Does the reorder require you to start where you left off?

13. Have you confirmed all details of your mailing list order including delivery date, in writing?

▪ 3 TIMES 7 ▪

Based on ideas from Bob Stone, here are 3 groups of 7 points, each designed to help you make your audience selection easier and better.

Considering House, Response, and Compiled Lists

First are 7 points to think about when you consider the lists we've just discussed:

1. Your house list will outpull all other lists.
2. A response list will outpull a compiled list.
3. People over 35 years old are more likely to be mail-order buyers.
4. Rural areas and small towns will give a greater response than urban areas in both business and consumer markets.
5. Geography *does* matter. You will get a different response from different postal codes, states, and regions; from SIC codes and all other measures.
6. Multiple buyers are more likely to buy from you than those who only bought once in the past, whether business or consumer.
7. Season matters. All things have a season. Halloween is October 31. None of us are going to change that. Sometimes we make more of season than is necessary; in many cases, the difference between the best and worse time is less than 20%. Yet don't forget season.

Evaluating the Options

Here are 7 points to consider when evaluating the options you have to selecting the right audience for you, your product, and your offer:

1. What is the universe of the list you are considering? How many names are on it? Find out in the beginning.
2. How old is the list—is it as current as you need it to be? When was the last time it was cleaned and updated?
3. What is the duplication factor, if any, and does it matter to you?

4. Is "hot line" selection (most current, active responders) available, and do you care (does it affect your offer)?
5. What available selection factors are important to you? For the consumer market, demographic and geographic? What other selections? What is the cost of this selection, and is it worth the extra cost?
6. Are telephone and fax numbers available; if so, at what additional cost? What about e-mail? For a fully integrated direct response program you very well may find all this data helpful. Know from the start if you can buy extra specifics as well as the base name.
7. What format is available—tape or disk, peel-off labels, cheshire labels? What other production questions do you know are important?

Ordering the List

The last group of 7 things to do when ordering your mailing list:

1. Always test before you buy big. Usually you test 5,000 or 10,000 names, then multiply that 5 times. If that result holds, multiply by 5 again. For example, you test and mail 10,000, then test 50,000, and then 250,000. There is no magic to this. Sometimes you roll out after the initial test; sometimes you continue testing smaller numbers before the big push.

2. Test segments as well as the whole. You will find both areas you wish to avoid and areas of pure gold within the same list.

3. Plan enough up-front time early in your program to allow for thorough audience evaluation, selection, and ordering. All else can go well, yet if you send your marvelous offer to the wrong audience, it will not work. Plan ahead.

4. Select your list by the quality you want, not quantity or price. If it is big and wrong, it is still wrong. If it is FREE and wrong, it cost too much! If it is $1.00 a name and it earns you a profit, it is the right list and could very well be a bargain.

5. When your list comes, look at it! Make sure it is what you ordered (and that includes your house list from your data processing department). People have been known to make mistakes. Only by looking at it can you be sure that it is correct.

6. Whatever your results, share them with everyone involved. This means your entire creative team, the production crew, your own staff, any and all outside suppliers, the list broker or manager, the printer, the consultant, the agency—everyone. They all have an interest and will work with you to make the next effort even better. Share results.

7. Test, test, test frequently. Continue your search for new audiences. Mail frequently. Repetition builds your reputation; frequency earns results.

If you don't already have profile information in your database customer file, get it. Do a telephone or direct mail survey. If you feel it will help, offer an advertising specialty up front for the data you need, or a premium on the back end, or both. Get the knowledge that will help you make your best offer to your best audience.

Get your key questions answered. Information is available. You need to obtain it to be able to specifically target market your audience. The idea is to find and take all information that is available on the people who buy and the companies that buy, match this information with your offer and needs, and do a chase (i.e., become as knowledgeable as possible, and use your knowledge). You may elect to use a variety of sources: lists for direct mail, telephone, fax, and e-mail campaign marketing; magazines and newspapers for print and space campaigns; radio and television for broadcast programming.

And then you AFTO—Ask for the Order!

■ MARKETS WITHIN MARKETS ■

Direct marketing has a host of definitions. There is much disagreement, even among the so-called experts and professionals, as to how to define direct marketing. All of them do agree that one of the key benefits of direct response is its ability to segment a marketplace in order to reach it more effectively with a message.

Segmentation is the key in direct response marketing. You will find markets within markets, smaller pockets within larger bases, and some of these will be unbelievably profitable. How do you find these golden groups? How do you gather these appropriate audiences together for your special product or service offer? How do you pinpoint those persons who will be most receptive to your marketing effort? You segment!

Markets and customers are in a constant state of flow and change. Products come and go. People do, too. Your customers today may not be there tomorrow. Because this is true, market segmentation is necessary. Segmentation has a purpose. It can provide an improved level of individual service to your clients to more accurately meet their needs. It can provide a higher level of satisfaction. All these benefits you offer your customers should be done with increased PROFIT to you.

(A word of caution about segmentation from good friend and copywriter supreme Herschell Gordon Lewis. Herschell reminds us of the danger of absolute targeting: "By saying, 'I know who you are,' if you're wrong, the message is ludicrous!")

The Prospecting Challenge

Everyone would like more new business. Those who are successful in getting it do so because they plan it that way. Here are 9 ways to be good at prospecting:

1. Aim your arrow at the right audience. Identify who your best prospects are and talk to them. Usually your most profitable prospecting results will come if you select your audience in this order:
   a. Your current customers
   b. Your former customers

    c. Your chief competitors' customers

    d. Look-alikes of your current customers

    e. Buyers of a product or service in a similar category to yours

2. Use an effective appeal, make a good offer; give your prospective audience a reason to listen to your message.

3. "Hold" your audience—be interesting, informative, useful, and maybe even entertaining. Make an outstanding presentation of your copy and art.

4. Promise all your benefits. Let your prospect know what good things will happen by doing business with you. And by doing it now.

5. Make your story believable, tell it like it is. However, make sure your prospect will understand and believe you.

6. Prove that what you have to offer (your product or service) is the best bargain going. Address it to the prospect's NEEDS and provide testimonials and case histories to prove your point.

7. Make it easy to reply for more information, to see a salesperson, to buy! Give complete order information; use a toll-free number, business response envelope, or card. Give a fax response option. Allow your prospect to reach you through the Web.

8. Give a reason to act now; your offer and benefits must present a reason for your audience to make a move to what you are selling, and to do it now.

9. Then, and this is most important, repeat your complete story all over again. Retell it to those who missed your message the first time around.

6 Marketing Concepts

Here is a series of 6 directly related marketing concepts. They will help you segment your market, analyze your prospects and customers, and understand their behavior and attitudes toward you and your products. These are the who, what, why, when, where, and how of direct marketing:

- **Who**—the organization or individual who buys the product
- **What**—the product, which is defined as what is purchased
- **Why**—the objective, which is the reason the product is purchased
- **When**—timing, which is when the product is bought
- **Where**—channel of distribution, which is where the product is bought
- **How**—the method of operation, which is how the product is purchased

Getting answers to even some of these questions will help you reach your customer base with a greater level of success.

5 Reasons for Segmentation

There are 5 primary reasons that market segmentation benefits your direct marketing program.

Reason 1: Adding Competitive Advantages

By segmenting, you are adding a competitive advantage to your product or service. You "specialize" in an area. You are the expert. You dive deeper and do it better than anyone else. You respond faster. You are more accurate. You understand opportunities and can react accordingly. You pinpoint an audience. You target an account. For example, our population is growing fastest in the over-55 age group. Within this area of specialization/segmentation, publications such as *Prime Time Tennis* and *Golf for Seniors* have a place in the market. These 2 magazines are aimed at very specific special-interest groups—segmentation at its finest.

Here is another example. Unisys is making its mark in specific fields with a focused approach. It has segmented the marketplace and reaches prospects with materials and a staff that "think" like the customer. Bankers sell to bankers; food service specialists sell to the packaged goods industry.

Here is a definition of market segmentation according to the DuPont Company: "A group of customers anywhere along the distribution chain who have common needs and values . . . who will respond similarly to our offering, and who are large enough to be strategically important to our business." Notice the key elements of that definition:

1. Common needs *and* values. This is most important. Lots of folks need things. To some they are worth more than others.

2. Respond similarly to our offering. This can only be shown when you make offers over and over on a continuing basis and measure what happens. One time is not a test; you need to take at least 3 shots at your audience, sometimes many more, before you know what is similar between your customers.

3. Strategically important. This says DuPont is the type of company ready to buy in relationship to the customer's needs and goals. That is, what the company buys will help you meet your objectives. So, they are most important to your plans.

Reason 2: Identifying New Markets

This is not obvious. The reason is that on the surface you often don't see these new market niches. They don't necessarily jump out at you. By segmenting your market, you can find new markets. They may be small, only in a few locations, very specific, or very particular.

Many times, what happens is that you start looking to reach outward—for example, to chief financial officers of major insurance corporations—and find you can use the same approach with those in manufacturing SIC code #31, Leather and Leather Products. Or you might select all the account supervisors working for CFOs in all Fortune 1,000 companies who, if not decision makers, are great influencers.

Segmenting can bring you additional market benefits.

Reason 3: Reducing Your Costs

Obviously, if you select carefully and only reach into the marketplace for a niche or specific segment your costs will be less. This applies to all media, particularly direct mail and telephone marketing. With these tools, list costs represent a large part of segmentation.

Saving on lists is only the beginning. Production is a major part of all marketing campaigns. It includes paper, printing, and letter-shop for direct mail; people and time for telemarketing; and fulfillment packages for all media.

If you don't have as many mailings or calls, you most certainly enjoy large savings. Being selective not only makes money, it saves money.

Reason 4: Reducing Credit Risks

You get a handle on credit. As unfortunate as it is true, there are folks and companies out there who don't pay their bills. Fortunately, not many of them; but still, enough to make the bravest financial officer quake on occasion. Using market segmentation allows you to eliminate those who cause credit problems or handle them as "cash only." You can reduce bad debt ratios and cut cancellations. On the positive side, you can offer extended credit terms to customers who have earned a good rating with you.

Only by segmenting your market into units do you have these options. In short, you can truly manage your markets, both business and consumer.

Reason 5: Purging Lists

By eliminating suspects who have a lesser probability of buying from you today and concentrating solely on those prime prospects who are most likely to turn into customers soon, your marketing efforts will bring rewards more quickly and at a higher profit level. The opportunity for second and continuing orders also comes faster.

With speed of sales comes a lowering of costs. You don't need the extra time to sell. Instead, you begin profitable service immediately, which reduces your costs. These savings fall to the bottom line and become those very nice increased profits.

The segmentation theory says the people most likely to buy from you are exactly like those who are already buying from you. It is relatively easy to divide markets into 2 main groups: those that buy, and those that do not.

As with any theory, it is easier to talk about it on paper than it is to perform in the marketplace. Your current customers have specific needs, desires, concerns, wants, expressions, feelings, needs. Your product gives satisfaction. Others who have similar needs, desires, concerns, wants, expressions, and more are very likely to also find satisfaction in your product or service if you will only ask them to buy, to become your customer.

The 7 Deadly Pitfalls of Segmentation

Here are 7 things to avoid or be careful of when doing market segmentation:

- Not randomly selecting samples
- Not creating back-end measurement files
- Waiting too long before rollout
- Not remarketing tested audiences
- Changing the universe between the test and the campaign
- Not considering variations in creative and offers
- Not accounting for geographic differences

Let's look at each of the pitfalls more closely.

Pitfall 1: Not Randomly Selecting Samples to Study

This is particularly dangerous. Sometimes in the excitement of major programs and campaigns, with the human desire to want winners, we forget that winning is not the purpose of segmentation. The purpose is to *find* winning groups—not make them.

A test sample must be representative of the total list. You want the results and your projections to be reliable. You want the promotion to work next time, too, when you roll out your program to the next level and the next.

Pitfall 2: Not Creating Back-End Measurement Files

Although measurement and analysis happen after you are in the marketplace, you must plan the process in the beginning. If you do not, you may forget such critical elements as match codes, which are vital to really learning what happened with your offer and your lists.

You must lay out on paper the math of your program—what you expect, your objectives, and when you'll break even. Then decide how to measure the levels of success. All this is done BEFORE going into the field. You may have several goals and thus several measures. That is fine, as long as you have them! Plan to apply your test results to the total campaign. Plan your measurement so you can measure your plan.

Pitfall 3: Waiting Too Long Before Rollout

The most carefully planned and well-executed programs will not pay off if there is too long a time between the test of the campaign and the campaign itself. Segments of the marketplace are fragile. Because they are smaller niches of the whole, they are more likely to change, and do so quickly. Sure, sometimes that is better for your program, but many times it is not!

The file is different when you go to it a second time, when you roll out your program. It has aged, it has moved, and it has heard from your competition. It is different. Take that sure fact into consideration. When you plan your test, plan your campaign in the beginning so you can take advantage of all opportunities promptly.

Pitfall 4: Not Remarketing Test Audiences

Some marketers feel the names you have tested should not be included in the rollout. I disagree. Almost without exception, there are more people on the list who did not respond than did. If the list as a whole worked, a repeat of your message to those test names is still worth a shot—a second shot and maybe more. On your second, third, and future mailings to this audience you may have a lower response rate because you creamed the list the first time. At the same time, you will gain more total response than if you had not chased this list again and again, over and over.

In most instances, you will gain more by repeat contacts with the same audience than by using a list only once. When you do chase them again, however, you must take that into account as you measure results. The reason is obvious: this group heard from you before. On this second contact, it is very likely whatever awareness and image levels you sparked previously and whatever interest you generated, you will reinforce.

Take into account the test group; measure it separately.

Pitfall 5: Changing the Universe Between the Test and the Campaign

Why this happens is a mystery, but it does. You carefully select and test a segmented audience. It works. Then you change the selection criteria when you roll out and wonder why the results fail to relate! Don't do that. This does not mean you should not test again some other or different collection of factors. Fine, test. Just don't expect the same results. The key word here is TEST.

When you find a profitable segment, go at it. At the same time, you can continue to test to improve the outcomes. Just don't mix it all together and expect the same results.

Pitfall 6: Not Considering Variations in Creative and Offers

As with all testing, you should do it for the look and content of your offer. Direct response marketing is founded on and succeeds with test, test, test. As in the audience testing recommended in Pitfall 5, you should expect different results.

If you change creative elements—the look, style, format, design, color, copy, anything and everything—you will get different results. This is fine, just make certain you know that is going to happen and be prepared.

When you change the offer from FREE to a 1 cent sale, free trial, limited time offer, or any variation, you will get different results. Expect them and measure accordingly.

Pitfall 7: Not Accounting for Geographic Differences

Birmingham is not Spokane. Maine is not Arizona. Albuquerque or Brisbane, Rome or Singapore or Toronto, east or west, north or south—geography does affect your results. These places are different, just as people are different.

Weather has a major impact on how people respond. When it is sunny on the beaches in Florida and raining on the streets of Boston, it is reasonable to expect any messages sent to your highly segmented audience in those two markets that day will be received differently. Expect that to happen, because it will.

Geography affects lifestyles. Even though you have a niche market, that niche is not 100% homogenous every day of the year. You are dealing with people—individual people—and they are all different.

▪ 3 VITAL QUESTIONS: WHO? WHERE? WHAT? ▪

Initially you identify your market, your audience segment, in terms of:

- Demographics, population characteristics, or WHO they are
- Geography, physical/location characteristics, or WHERE they are
- Psychographics, lifestyle characteristics, or WHAT they think

Segmentation has these 3 main groups of information. Let's talk about them one by one.

Demographics—the Who Factor

First is demographics. Who are these people you want to reach? Are you looking at business or consumer markets?

Business Demographics

For business markets, there are many different parts to demographics. As mentioned earlier, you talk to individuals, even when selling business-to-business. Real, live, down-to-earth people. Most of these individuals have a title that helps you understand their job description. A title is important because it begins to provide you with some information about your audience. It helps with classification of your prospects. In some instances, a title is as important as a name (almost—having the *correct* name is always best), because a name may not be available. With changes, promotions, and the like, keeping up with a name for prospecting purposes is often not worth the time, effort, or expense.

Titles come many different ways. They could be exactly as the industry you're addressing defines them. They could be a series of titles that cross a number of industries. They could be descriptive. Here are some possible titles within certain groups:

Group	Title
Large company	Vice president
Branch office, midsize company	General manager
Secondary school	Superintendent
Local government	Administrative manager
Church	Pastor
Mall retailer	Owner or manager

Descriptive titles work because you direct your message by function, by responsibility, with little chance for error. A descriptive title such as "the person in charge of shipping to and from Puerto Rico," "the executive in charge of buying trucks," or "the person in charge of the photocopy machine" will help you reach the right audience. This type of direction almost guarantees your direct mail message will get to someone with responsibility. If you telephone a company and ask a question using one of these descriptions, you'll most likely be routed to someone who can answer your question. Your direct marketing campaign can work the same charm. Get to the person you want.

Demographics for business include a lot more as well. As mentioned earlier under profiling your customer base, the Standard Industrial Classification codes can be important. What are SIC codes? They are a system for identifying different types of business. The broad groups are as follows:

Agriculture	Manufacturers	Retailers
Forestry	Transportation	Finance
Fishing	Communications	Insurance
Construction	Wholesalers	Business
Professional	Government	services
services	offices	

Within each of these groupings, selection is available by many factors, including sales dollar volume, financial standing, net worth, years in business, number of offices, headquarters or branch locations, number of employees, geography, and many more. You can select by city size if that is important. Choose by companies that do Yellow Pages advertising versus those that do not, which titles within which departments of the same company give you the best chance at an appointment or order, and dozens of combinations of these and other factors.

Business marketing has more decision makers than consumer offers. For business, you could be talking to a half dozen or more people before a major buying decision is made. These are the people you need to reach with your message if you are to be successful. Sometimes the same person wears several hats, particularly in a smaller company. Sometimes in larger firms, there is a committee that "sits."

At times, many different people in the same department of the same company need to get your message. They may have similar titles in different divisions. It might be best to send different messages to the CEO, CFO, general manager, purchasing agent, and group supervisor. Different messages—same offer. Playing each message to the needs of that person's responsibilities.

In almost every instance in business-to-business, multiple contacts will be necessary. Not a one-shot advertisement in a specific trade journal or one piece of direct mail, but many messages to many people. That's what works best, once you've clearly defined your target audience.

Consumer Demographics

Demographics for the consumer are not nearly as complex, yet there are many options. In the profile section of this chapter, we mentioned a number of these traits. The Census Bureau has "averages" by census tract and postal code (also finer cuts in some instances and larger groupings as well). In the United States, there are approximately 150 census characteristics available to select from, including income by household, ethnic background, profession or occupation, religious background, head of household, new movers, retirees, age, gender, renters or homeowners, and vehicle owners (including motor homes, motorcycles, trucks, and cars).

Larger consumer lists are usually compiled with a combination of data—from automobile registrations, telephone listings, census tract information, and more. One national firm uses 19 sources, merging over 325 million records annually, to come up with one list of households.

Figure 5.1 shows the influence of demographics on a product. In this example, 5 characteristics are deemed significant. It is quickly obvious only 3 are extremely important:

- **Gender.** Females buy more than 2:1 over males.
- **Marital status.** Married people buy more than 3:1 over single people.
- **Race.** Caucasians buy by 3:1 over all other races combined.

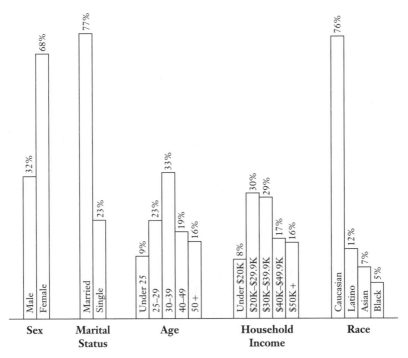

Figure 5.1 ▪ 5 Demographics for a Particular Consumer Product

Age and household income are important, but not as much as the other elements.

Many other factors also may be important; for example, media buying areas, which have changed greatly with the influence of cable, satellites, and more recently the World Wide Web. Newspaper distribution networks also may be important in audience selection. Larger city and national papers (*The Wall Street Journal, The New York Times, USA Today*) that cover a state or region certainly have a different impact than smaller weeklies.

There also are belts: economic belts, the Farm Belt, and the Bible Belt. And then there is the Sun Belt, with its "snowbirds"—people who live in cooler climates during the summer, and at the first sign of real winter flee the cold and head to the desert and beaches for the rest of the year. Sure, belts could be classified under geography because they represent a series of characteristics of a group of people who just happen to be in an area. I elect to place them with demographics, because we're talking about people.

Generally, success in audience selection for consumer and business comes from a combination of types and sources of lists. It is unlikely there is any single, best source that will give optimal performance. You need to select, test, and use a variety until you find the right combination that works best for you and suits your sales requirements.

Geography—the Where Factor

Geography definitely affects your audience selection for both consumers and business. Fast-food restaurants and branch banking have a radius of approximately 3 miles. They draw 80%–85% of their customers because they are convenient and close. Why is this the case? Because in urban and suburban areas you don't need to go any farther than 3 miles to get service. Plus, you have selection.

On the other hand, you will drive farther for an evening out at a fine supper club, for a play or movie, for a night at the ball game or a day at an amusement park.

Sometimes postal codes will define where you go for service. A railroad crossing, a freeway interchange, a river, or any major man-made or natural "change" in the landscape has a great effect on consumer marketing.

The local newspaper service area dictates where you put your advertisements as a business and where your customers come from. Radio and television stations' signal area determines how you use broadcast, who your prospects are, and whether or not you can get business. Superstations and cable have changed that somewhat, but only if you have national distribution and/or your product can be sold via mail order.

As mentioned earlier, there are a number of belts across the country corresponding to such factors as sun, iron, farms, snow, economics (which vary and shift a lot more than those tied to weather and nature), politics, and religion.

Towns, cities, counties, valleys, states, and regions all help you decide where your marketing message goes. If your product or service is unique or different, people will travel farther to get it. If it is a commodity, it must be close to the home or office or easy to buy over the telephone, through the mail, or on the Web.

Telephone and credit cards, electronic mail, facsimiles, telexes, and other communication tools have greatly expanded the geographic limits of many products and services for consumers and businesses. The mail-order industry is booming because it is easy to place an order 24 hours a day for almost anything.

It is not always necessary to have a storefront operation to be successful in business—certainly not for businesses using direct marketing as a channel of distribution. You name it, and it has been sold using direct response techniques: money by mail ($25,000 offered by one company), office and computer supplies, electronic gear, measuring instruments, and other high-tech equipment costing hundreds or even thousands of dollars. Training aids, such as tapes, CDs, and books, and other business tools bring in from under $100 to many thousands of dollars on one order. Even plumbing supplies are sold this way—one company I know sells spa, hot tub, and jet bath nuts and bolts with an average order of over $650. You can buy clothes from head to toe—any size, color, shape, or style—at almost any price. One company accepts a trade-in of your old work shoes on a new pair! Order thick steaks and the knives to cut them, china to serve them on and the silver to eat them with.

Geography offers no bounds in mail order. If anything, the boundaries have expanded even more with access to the Web. The Web gets your message to your audience. They choose to order online or through a toll-free phone or fax line. Payment is with a credit card. Shipment is via overnight delivery service—postal service, FedEx, UPS, DHL, and the like.

When you clearly identify your right audience, you can sell by direct response. Some products and product lines do not work in mail order. Still, direct response can be important to their sales success. How? By developing a lead generation or traffic building program.

So far, most systems for business, such as computer networks and telephone equipment, work best when you feel, touch, and see them work. Sure, there are the techies who are comfortable with a box arriving on their doorstep. Dell, Gateway, and others sell tens of millions of dollars of equipment each week via the Web and over the telephone to those who do NOT need touch-feel. Not me! So, lead generation does and will continue to work for those of us who need hand-holding.

Almost anything that is extremely heavy is best sold retail, where a traffic building program with a special offer to get you into the store will work. Low-profit/low-margin items, everyday items that are available almost everywhere, are not good products for mail order. Ice cream is tough, yet your local independent or franchisee store can still mail you a coupon to get you in the front door (traffic building). The unusual will work. Not long ago, I purchased 2 gallons of matzo ball soup from a deli in Brooklyn and had it shipped to a friend in Santa Monica, California.

Geography is important where personalized sales and service are important. Small television sets can be sold using direct response mail order. What about service on your big screen?

Because most art and decorative items for the home and office are both expensive and heavy, pure mail order rarely works. However, catalogs are used to "show and tell" the potential buyer all the options.

Will you drive 250 miles to buy a home entertainment center or groceries? Probably not, because you don't have to; it is too inconvenient. You can get both sales and service closer to home. Will you call a toll-free number to order an inexpensive 5-inch handheld television? Sure you will, it's easy to do. The product is unusual enough that it isn't in every store, and it doesn't cost so much you might be concerned.

Traffic building programs for both business and consumer retail stores and for consumer and industry-specific trade shows are all a major part of direct response marketing, with heavy use of direct mail, broadcast (usually radio for business and both radio and television for consumer), and print (newspapers more than magazines). The media selected directly relate to the geography of the event and its worth and value in the buyer's mind against the time and cost.

Psychographics—the What Factor

"I love gardening, gourmet foods, beautiful music, gift-giving, computing, decorating—but I have a passion for fashion!" Educational background; behavior and attitudes; previous experiences; hobbies; activities related to the home and/or office; and memberships in associations, clubs, and church all affect how you think and what you will do. They affect what you own, such as the number of computers in your home, the number of homes, the art you collect, your yacht, how many and what type of cars. They influence whether you have a beeper, cell phone, or both; the number and type of credit cards you use, whether you are a stockholder or own real estate; whether you travel around the world or stay home. Your social, political, and religious life all impact your decisions.

On the business front, your lifestyle is affected by such things as your profession and its image to the general public; whether you have an executive bathroom key, a corner office, a personal parking space, and a corporate platinum credit card; how many phones are on your desk; the plaques on your wall; even if you have your own Web site as part of your business place on the Internet. The associations in which you are active (including being on the board of directors), the charities to which you donate, and the clubs to which you belong all influence what you will do when urged to make a buying decision.

Psychographics is that extra dimension that allows for better audience identification and selection. It is especially helpful on the consumer side, because all buying decisions are made by people for people. And much of the personal data can be recorded. Database companies collect this information and make it available to consumer marketers.

On the business side, it is much more difficult to obtain true psychographics. People still make decisions; however, they make them with and for other people and companies. You can build your own database of information in the business category by talking with your customers and listening very carefully. Your telemarketers, your phone order desk, your outside sales representatives can all feed you information that will help. Your Web site can gather all sorts of interesting and helpful bits of data.

Once you have it, it may be difficult to match to outside lists when prospecting for new business, because so few psychographic characteristics are available from the business list community. Still, it can be very helpful in providing an extra detail of service or attention. Show a level of caring with your current customers.

The Cluster Principle

People with similar demographics and psychographic profiles tend to cluster in the same geographic areas (birds of a feather flock together). Companies do the same. There is a "restaurant row" in most cities. Some communities have the "automobile mile" where all the auto dealers cluster. The financial community—banks, brokerage houses, and insurance companies—does likewise.

Major cities have large ethnic communities where people from similar cultures live together. The same happens with religion. Churches, temples, and mosques go up in a community where people of the same faith need them. This does not happen by chance; it is planned.

There are collections of just about everything. This is an important fact to know when you go looking for that right audience to reach with your message. It helps you find, identify, and reach specific audiences by being able to capitalize on the Cluster Principle.

In business, using SIC codes, carefully combed to select the demographics, geographics, and even psychographics available, will help you select mom-and-pop shops versus Fortune 500 companies.

You can also apply the cluster approach within a geographic region to select the right audience. All of a certain set of characteristics in the 11 western U.S. states, or the Northeast, or the area south of Interstate 10 in southern California or adjacent to the Snake River in Idaho can be specified. Ditto for Western Europe, members of the EuroUnion, Southeast Asia, and elsewhere around the world.

My friend Jock Falkson notes that, interestingly enough, for many mail-order marketers and those in fund-raising, the Cluster Principle is not applicable. It is particularly unsuitable for consumer mail-order companies, which frequently find their audience widely scattered. Although the individuals have similar characteristics, they are not necessarily clustered in close or even similar geographic regions. They are a small part of the total populace and they are everywhere. They do not always group together.

For lead generation programs, the Cluster Principle can and does work. For traffic building programs, it is almost mandatory. When you select your prospects within any or all of a set of similar parameters, it will help you get your message to the right audience.

∎ 11 AUDIENCE IDEAS TO REMEMBER ∎

Here is a laundry list of 11 thoughts to remember and use according to your situation. Not for you to ADOPT, but rather for you to ADAPT to your particular and special needs.

1. Clearly define and refine your market, your audience, BEFORE you begin your creative processes. Define all the belts and "graphics" in the beginning. Make certain your reference materials and statistics are no more than 12 months old. Know your audience.

2. Many times, occupational segmentation to a target audience can work. Categories should be specific, such as electrical engineers

versus all engineers, fast-food restaurants versus all restaurants, trial lawyers versus all lawyers, plumbing contractors versus general contractors, dentists versus the health care field, and independent insurance agents versus insurance companies. The same goes for departments within companies. If you want to communicate with the personnel department, make certain your message indicates they are your audience.

3. Understand that business marketing and consumer marketing are different. Also, remember in both that you are talking to people—individuals, not companies. Talk to your audiences, all of them, as people. Talk with them one-on-one.

4. Without a doubt, a name is better than a title, but only if it is the right name! If you do not have a name or are unsure of the accuracy of the one you have, get it. Or use a title. Title addressing works for both business and consumer marketing.

5. Change titles when you change industry or level of contact. Talk to your audiences in their language. Don't talk down; don't talk up, either. Talk to them eye-to-eye. Using the correct titles for a specific industry group will let your audience know you took the time to care.

6. Know you have scores of selections and options. Be innovative in your selection of best audiences. Go to more than one source. Mix and match until, through testing, you are comfortable that you have the best combination. Then, roll it out and keep on testing!

7. Buy the best list, not the biggest or the least expensive. The best list will get you the best results. Anything less won't work as well. Your successes will come because you talked to the right audience, not because you talked to lots of people.

8. Don't be concerned about some duplication on your mailing list. In most situations, duplication won't hurt—in fact, it might help. Your audience will grow because your package will be routed to others. This is not always true for consumer marketing, but it most certainly is for business. Measure results in ORDERS, not numbers of packages mailed or number of duplications. Only orders count.

9. Know who does NOT respond and find out why not. If you can, change, alter, correct, and enhance your offer and hit that group

again—and again. If not, drop them and go on with others where your success ratio is higher. You will not score every time. Neither do the greats in any sport—basketball, soccer, or baseball.

10. Plan in the beginning to track your results in the end. Make it measurable from day one. Make certain all the research you've done up front gets measured on the back end. Know what you want and need to know to ensure a profitable program. Then measure against those goals.

11. Try old ideas again. Save new ideas and try them in the future. There is no such thing as a bad idea, just one whose time hasn't come. Bring back the old audience ideas you had in the past and didn't test; try them. Retest those that came close to working, see if you can get them on track. And don't throw away ideas you have now just because they don't fit today. Add color, spice. Turn them inside out, upside down, backward, and over. Add, subtract, multiply, divide. Give your "new" idea the old college try. Do it again. Mix 'em. Match 'em. And do it again.

Power direct marketing is selecting from these 11 "rules" and adapting those that fit your needs. By doing so, you'll do a better job at selecting the right audience for your product or service.

Chapter 6

OFFER

How 50% Off Makes You Feel 100% Better—Guaranteed!

■ ■ ■

Power direct marketing includes Offer as the fifth point of The 8ight Point Market Action Plan. The purpose of an offer is to communicate the benefits of doing business with you so your audience will give you an order.

■ Some Questions to Consider ■

Here are some questions to consider as you plan your offer:

1. Who are your competitors, and what are they offering?
2. What are your unique selling propositions (USPs)? Today, some experts say PoD—point of difference or point of distinction—same idea. So, what are yours, and your prime competition's? What are your weaknesses? Your competition's weaknesses?
3. How does your price compare with your competition's? Competitive, discount, premium, or even a mix?

4. Is an incentive or premium desired or needed to capture sales?
5. What is the product motivation to move a prospect to become a customer?
6. How does the customer benefit from using your product? What benefits do you offer prospects?
7. What does market research say about the position of your product? Can it be improved? Varied? Redirected? How can you best communicate your message to your prime prospective audience?
8. Why should anybody be interested in your product (be honest)? Why should they buy yours instead of somebody else's? Why should they buy anything at all from you today?

Americans make up only 6% of the earth's population, yet consume nearly 60% of the world's advertising. Television, radio, outdoor, magazines, newspapers, the World Wide Web, direct mail, the telephone, the fax machine, and e-mail attack our minds each day using millions of words, sounds, and pictures. Every day we are exposed to 570 advertising and marketing messages. So, how can you break through this so-called "clutter"? *With a clean, clear, and interesting offer!*

An offer is a reason for talking to your prospective audience. Just as a personal sales call needs a reason for happening, so must your marketing message have a reason for being. An offer helps you be successful.

A weak or poor message or offer to the right audience has a chance of bringing some success. It does not work the other way around. The right offer to the right audience is essential for prime response and superior results.

In all cases of communication with your public, one sales principle must be remembered: It is not what you have to sell; it's what the customer wants to buy. You need to present your case, no matter who you are: a bank, an insurance firm, a furniture store, an airline, a fast-food restaurant, a distributor or dealer, a service organization, a manufacturing company, a fund-raiser, a computer store, or a utility—whether you sell business-to-business or business to the consumer.

Give your prospects what they NEED and turn them into customers. Or, as my dad taught me long ago, find out what your customers need and give it to them. Make them an offer. Show and tell your prospect, through the creative approach, the benefits of doing business with you.

You must remember the market you are talking to is not necessarily turned on to learning about another way to do something. They weren't thinking of buying now or investing in a new idea, even yours, today. So, the copy must be:

- Quick
- To the point
- Easy to understand
- In a clear, **BOLD** typeface
- Using hard-hitting graphics

Make your decisions on the marketplace by what you perceive your prospect wants to hear and see. Know your audience! Make your offer to that audience.

■ RELATING OFFERS TO OBJECTIVES ■

Before you choose the most appropriate way to offer your products or services, you must be absolutely clear about the objectives to be achieved. These are questions that need to be answered:

- Are you trying to win new customers?
- If so, what can you afford to spend to secure each new order?
- How many customers have to renew their commitment or purchase again to make the program viable?

If you concern yourself only with the cost per inquiry or cost per original order, you may run into trouble on customer reactivation or on renewal. You must look at *both* the short-term and the long-term implications of the way you structure your offers. Once you are confident, or have evidence from tests, that you have the right offer, you should make it as attractive to prospects as you possibly can.

■ A Score and More Ways to Make Your Offer ■

Offers can be presented many different ways. Your response will change depending on not only what your offer is, but how it is presented. For instance, here are three ways to say basically the same thing: 1/2 price; 50% off; buy one, get one FREE. All 3 are very similar—not exactly alike, but similar. And yet they "sound" extremely different. Depending on how you use them, your offer will be understood or not.

Here is another example: save 25%; buy 9—get 3 FREE. Again, 2 ways to say the same thing. Many times, a retailer or distributor selling supplies will do a "buy 9, get 3 free"—buy 9 dozen pencils and get 3 dozen free. It works. Why does it work? Because you were considering buying 6 dozen pencils. Yet, with an offer like "buy 9, get 3 free," how can you refuse the extra savings? This is not to say that sometimes a straight 25% off isn't better. Sometimes it is; sometimes it is not.

A third example is: FREE trial versus money-back guarantee. Really, they're the same thing. In one case, you get a free trial before you pay. In the other, you pay up front and have a money-back guarantee. They are different; yet they are the same.

And, one more example: 25¢ a day; $7.50 a month; and $90.00 a year. These 3 ways of defining an amount are equal: 25¢ a day equals $7.50 a month equals $90.00 a year. Which sounds better to you? Which is the better way to talk about how much the product is going to cost you? It depends; yet 25¢ is so little (less than the cost of a cup of coffee anywhere in the world), almost anyone could afford this low price and can easily relate the small cost to the benefits of the offer.

Here are a few more offers selected from magazines, newspapers, and direct mail packages:

- 100% double tax free—a financial offer
- 100% fat free—a nutritional offer
- During summer, save 20% on slides—an offer made to me by a slide manufacturer/producer. (He knows I use many images in my seminar presentations. During the summer, his business is slow. It is a good offer for both of us.)
- One size fits all—a clothing manufacturer's sweatshirt offer
- Custom tailoring—special offer from a Hong Kong tailor
- The 15-minute loan now available from these convenient locations—an offer from the Bank of Boston. (It asks the prospect to call from any telephone, anywhere, at any time. Your loan application will be accepted over the telephone, and they'll process it in 15 minutes. A very good offer.)

What is it that will make the prospect take some action? Your offer must be perceived as having value to your prospect.

Make the most attractive offer you can make:

1. Free catalog
2. Free booklet with helpful information
3. Premium allied to your service
4. Free demonstration
5. Free survey and estimate
6. Special pricing or package
7. Free trial offering
8. Full and unconditional guarantee
9. Buy 1, get 1 free
10. Volume discount
11. Free gift (not a bribe)

12. Newsletter, free *x* times a year
13. Short-term introductory offer
14. Money-back guarantee

Use involvement devices, such as

- peel-offs
- rubouts
- yes, no, and maybe stickers
- tear-here order forms
- perforations
- stubs
- samples, if your product lends itself to sampling

Test them. They work for consumer and business markets, mail and space advertising. They are creative approaches that work to get action on your offer. Testing 2 (or more) totally and completely different creative packages and offers will help you learn what will sell best for you.

In developing the creative approach for your offer, think about these questions:

1. Will what you offer make the purchaser feel more important?
2. Will it make the purchaser happier?
3. Will it make the purchaser comfortable?
4. Will it make the purchaser prosperous?
5. Will it make the purchaser's work easier?
6. Will it make the purchaser feel more secure?
7. Will it make the purchaser attractive or better liked?
8. Will it provide the purchaser with some distinction?
9. Will it appeal to the purchaser as a bargain?

The offer must be outstanding. A small percentage of your prospects will buy from you no matter what you say or how you say it. A large number (usually over 90%) won't give you the time of day, no matter how good or attractive your offer may be. The difference between these 2 groups is where it's at! It's where you'll make it or not. Make your offer to the fence-sitters. Get them to roll to your side.

An example of a good offer is a story from Japan. Many of you have visited Japan and traveled to see 12,389-foot Mount Fuji. It is one of those interesting mountains; it stands alone. It is not part of a range; it is a solo peak. Consequently, it makes its own weather. Many times, you can't see the mountain from the base. It is foggy and rainy and the cloud cover is so low you can't see the mountain itself. Since most people go to the Mount Fuji area to see the mountain, they are obviously disappointed if they can't. At the base of the mountain, there are a number of lakes. On each of the lakes is a small inn. The owner of one of these inns has come up with an excellent offer. If you come to Mount Fuji and stay at his inn, any day you cannot see the mountain you do not have to pay your room rent. The room is FREE. This is an excellent offer. Think about it. You've gone on a trip to see the mountain. You're disappointed because you can't. Here is an innkeeper who recognizes your plight and is doing something about it. You are a winner! At the same time, the inn wins, too. Why? Because 1 or both of the following things normally happen:

- Because you've gotten the night free, you decide to stay another night. After all, you had planned on spending that money anyway.
- You can't stay another night, so you spend the money another way. You go to the finest restaurant in the inn, rather than the coffee shop. You sit in the bar and drink sake. You go to the inn gift shop and spend money you weren't going to spend. You decide to have a sauna and a massage.

You get the idea. The inn wins because it has made an excellent offer to you. You win by getting some benefits you didn't plan on.

This is an example of a perfect offer. An offer is not designed to give the store away. The offer is designed to move more merchandise or services and to provide a reward to the customer for doing business with you at this time. The idea is each side gains from the exchange—WIN-WIN!

You want me to buy? Make me an offer I can't refuse.

▪ How to Test Your Offer ▪

If you've prepared a break-even budget or a profit and loss forecast, taking great care with the relevant details, you know exactly what response you need from your promotion to be successful, profitable. The response target is simply the minimum figure you are prepared to accept from your promotion. Knowing what this figure is and actually achieving it or bettering it are different matters.

You may feel, based on your experience, that the response is bound to exceed quota. On the other hand, you may not be at all confident the results will exceed your targeted response rate. Either way, you can virtually eliminate the risk of an expensive flop by conducting a prepromotion test to establish what the response rate is likely to be.

In effect, direct mail testing is a form of market research. The results can be a reliable guide to what you may expect, because direct mail tests are similar to full-scale promotions. With direct mail testing, you have the distinct advantage of almost total control of distribution. This means you select samples from the market universe (the mailing or telemarketing list) in the quantities you require and in a fashion that produces a valid, representative sample.

In testing it is important to concern yourself and your project with only the BIG differences. Test the need-to-know things first. Save those that would be nice to know for a later time.

Here are some of the many types of things you can test:

Product features and benefits
Price
Discount plans
Copy approach
Gift certificates
Stuffers for other products
Lists
Fax marketing
Guarantees
Additional order forms
E-mail response
Back-end premiums or gifts
Testimonials
Outbound telemarketing
Age groups
Geography/marketplace
Methods of payment (cash,
   check, money order,
   purchase order, credit)

Contests, sweepstakes,
   drawings
Terms of service
Postage rate
Toll-free telephone service
Limited-time offers
New market categories
Credit terms
Warranties
Format, layout, design
Up-front advertising
   specialties
Case histories
Preferences by gender
Job functions
Seasons
Media: mail, fax, Web, space,
   phone, broadcast, and
   "other"

The Test Matrix

Let's first talk about what you CANNOT test. You cannot test the elements shown in Figure 6.1. Why not? Why can't you test a blue circle versus a yellow square versus a green triangle? Because if the blue circle wins, what wins? Blue or the circle? You don't know, so your test is invalid. You can test blue against green against yellow, or you can test triangles against circles against rectangles. Either will teach you something. The combination of a green triangle, a blue circle, and a yellow rectangle will not work.

Testing 2 or more totally different creative approaches, offers, lists, and/or other things will help you learn what will sell best. Figure 6.2 is an example of how you can test 2 direct mail packages—offers with and without premiums and 2 prices—at the same time and know the results following the test.

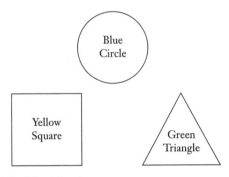

Figure 6.1 ■ The Test Matrix

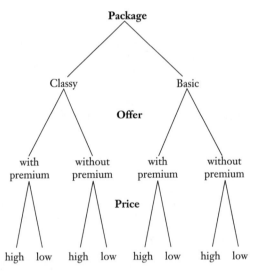

Figure 6.2 ■ Direct Mail Test Matrix

This matrix allows you to determine which direct mail package, the classy and upscale version or the more basic package, gains you the most response or the most return on investment. You also can decide whether offering the premium increases your response with quality or only numbers. Is it worth the extra cost? Finally, you can decide which of 2 price points works best toward getting your objectives fulfilled.

Some Things to Consider When Testing Mailing Lists

One of the primary things to test is lists—different segments of the same list, active names versus those on an inactive file. Look at those who responded most recently—sometimes called "hot line names"—versus others. Frequency of activity, level of activity, and type of product or service purchased will help you reach your best audience.

Here is a list of questions to answer as you consider and plan a mailing list test:

1. Where did this list come from, what is its source?
2. Is the sample a truly random sample?
3. Is the nth* name selection representative of the entire list, or of a special selection from within the whole?
4. Is the survey sample large enough to give you meaningful and measurable results?
5. Could the list have been "preheated"? That is, were there any outside factors that might affect your results?
6. Did the list owner or broker have any special reason for the selection method used?
7. Did all the lists included in the test belong in the test?
8. When you measured the results, were all the responses reported and counted?
9. Did you use percentages because the raw numbers looked bad?
10. Are the results consistent with previous results?
11. When you evaluated all the results, on what basis did the winner win?

---

*nth means a random selection from the total, such as every 5th, 10th, or 22nd name available from the total list.

Testing (numbers in thousands)

Packages \ Lists	#1	#2	#3	#4	Totals
A	5	2.5	5	2.5 / 2.5	17.5
B	5	2.5	5	2.5 / 2.5	17.5
Totals	10	5	10	10	35

Figure 6.3 ■ Sample Chart for Testing Mailing Lists and Packages Together

Testing mailing lists and offers *together* is important for both consumer and business programs so you can determine which lists pull best against which offer. Figure 6.3 is another chart showing how to test lists and offers together. In this sample, you have 2 offers and 4 mailing lists. By testing all possible combinations, you learn what works best.

In addition to testing 4 different lists against 2 different offers to determine which combination pulled best, a further offer test was made. Under list #4, a further split—testing a premium offer versus a nonpremium offer—was tried. This smaller number allows for evaluation before going to big numbers and possibly making a major mistake.

What do you gain from even simple tests such as these? You gain knowledge about your marketplace; what stops them to consider and/or order from you rather than from the competition. You learn what mailing list works best. You learn how much to invest in your direct mail and whether it will bring high-quality and profitable results. You learn bottom line whether direct response is a tool you can use! It is not the answer to every prayer. It won't solve every problem. For a relatively small investment, you can test and learn what your next step should be.

You test the best offer you can make to see whether it works, remembering all the time that there are no failures—only lessons.

Multimedia Testing

Can you test direct mail versus telephone versus bill inserts? What about various combinations of these direct response tools, and multiple contact verses a single approach? Can you test all of these things and learn anything useful? Sure you can!

Here's what happened with just such a test. A customer list was divided into 7 equal segments. The offer was the same to each; only the media and number of contacts were different. Here are the sales results:

Media	Response Rate
Telephone bill insert only	2.0%
Telemarketing contact only	5.3%
Direct mail package only	7.9%
Insert and telemarketing	9.0%
Insert and direct mail	9.2%
Direct mail and telemarketing	16.4%
All 3 (insert, direct mail, and telemarketing)	29.3%

Please do not dwell on the specific response rates. They are not important. They are only numbers. What IS important is the fact that several tools, working together over a period of time, directed to the same audience with the same offer, worked. With dramatic increases in results! This test clearly shows the power of direct response, particularly the integration of several tools used in harmony over a period of time, all toward the same goal.

■ Why People Buy ■

People, not companies, make buying decisions. I have never sold anything to a company, only a person. People are individuals and your message must be to people as individuals and not as a mass or a number.

In 1924, an anonymous author stated the 5 motives to buy were love, gain, duty, self-indulgence, and self-preservation. Today, they can be capsulated in 4 general motives:

- To be liked
- To be appreciated
- To be right
- To be important

The late Ed Mayer listed 26 reasons why people buy:

1. To make money
2. To save money
3. To save time
4. To avoid effort
5. To get more comfort
6. To achieve greater cleanliness
7. To attain fuller health
8. To escape physical pain
9. To gain praise
10. To be popular
11. To attract the opposite sex
12. To conserve possessions
13. To increase enjoyment
14. To gratify curiosity
15. To protect family
16. To be in style
17. To have or hold beautiful possessions

18. To satisfy appetite
19. To emulate others
20. To avoid trouble
21. To avoid criticism
22. To be individual
23. To protect reputation
24. To take advantage of opportunities
25. To have safety in buying something else
26. To make work easier

▪ THE OFFER CHART ▪

The offer chart (see Figure 6.4) provides a matrix for your company and your product together. Unique and Common refer to your product or service; Known and Unknown refer to your company or organization. *Unique* is just that: different, unusual, new, a large step forward. Many new product introductions in telecommunications

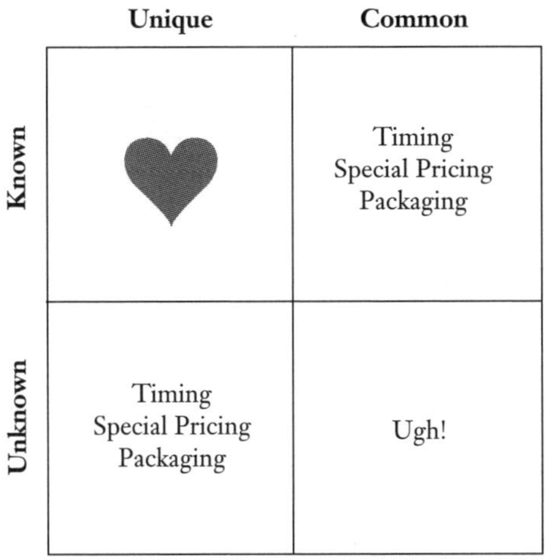

Figure 6.4 ▪ The Offer Chart

and technical fields begin as unique. Worldwide, every day, an average of 43 new consumer products are introduced. (Please note, I said consumer—this doesn't include business products!) That's over 15,600 each year. Even if what you have to offer is "new," you still have lots of competition.

A *common* item is something that is available through many sources, possibly a mature product in a mature marketplace. It is common and taken for granted. Anything that can be classified as "supplies" fits this classification, such as office supplies, computer supplies, or medical supplies.

Your company is *known* when it is a big player in its field. It may be a large fish in a small pond—you don't have to be internationally recognized to be known. Maybe you are known only in a geographic region.

Unknown means you are not yet well known. You may be a start-up; maybe you're number 5 or 8 or 12 on a list of companies in this same field. It doesn't mean you don't have anything to offer. It does mean you are a lesser player in this product or service category.

If you are known and your product is unique, you have a "sweetheart" situation. Your offer may be only that you are the leader in the field. You are first. You offer more than any of the competition. Sometimes this will work if you are known *and* your product is unique.

If you are unknown, you must have a sound, clear offer even if you have a unique product. An offer needs to take into consideration the timing of the introduction, the packaging of the product, its price, and possibly first-time specials. What if you are unknown and your product is common, sometimes called a commodity? Ugh! But you may still find it profitable to be in your business, provided you have offers reflecting what is happening in the marketplace, your launch is timed right, it is bundled or packaged accordingly, it is priced correctly, and it offers a special inducement to the end user over and above the product benefits. If you offer a common product or service, you might consider how to position it according to the thinking of Neil Cannon, chairman and CEO of Schmidt-Cannon. He suggests four ideas for selling commodities:

- **Convenience.** You're easy to talk to. You're available.
- **Experience.** You've been around the track a few times. You know what you're talking about.
- **Reliability.** You do what you say you're going to do. You fulfill your promises.
- **Exclusivity.** How can you offer an "exclusive" commodity? Many products are those we use every day and don't think a thing about. YOU take the common, everyday item and turn it into something "special." You make a commodity unique by adding something to it. You make it different, you offer something over and above what your competition is doing. You make it exclusive.

An unknown company does not want to begin business selling common products. The only exception I can think of to this rule is if you can isolate a true niche marketplace and service it with products or services unique and special to that market. In that case, offering common could work well.

Let's go back to the early 1980s and the personal computer business. In which quadrant on the offer chart were PCs in 1980 through 1982? Well, IBM was in the Known/Unique square. The company was well known, and when it came out with the PC it was still a unique offering. Where are personal computers today? They are very definitely common, everyday buys, nothing special.

▪ PACKAGING AND THE OFFER ▪

Briefly, let's consider packaging and the offer. Here are some examples of products that enjoyed increased sales when packaging was changed to serve the marketplace:

- V-8 juice in cartons, similar to milk cartons, gained access to the refrigerator section of supermarkets. The result was a 15% jump in sales.

- Noxzema skin lotion is now available in a pump container to serve women with long fingernails who don't like jars.
- Nestlé changed its candy packaging from boxes to bags so stores would move them lower on the shelves where people see them.
- United Ad Label offered alternate packaging of its "stock" labels sold to hospitals, from a minimum of 1,000 per roll to 500. The result? The company recaptured much of the smaller hospital marketplace.

As James Moran of Campbell Soup says: "Packaging has become almost as important as the product itself."

The folks at Avon agree. Skin-So-Soft is the largest-selling skin cream in the world. In the 1980s, a different application for it surfaced. Skin-So-Soft became a fantastic seller as a mosquito repellent. Avon repackaged the product for this new use. As a direct result, its sales increased annually and continue to do so today. They probably always will, as long as mosquitoes are about.

You need to look at the offer chart, decide where you fit and what you need for your offer BEFORE you determine what your offer should be.

High Involvement/Low Involvement/Think/Feel

Foote Cone Belding (FCB), an international advertising, public relations, and direct marketing agency has prepared the offer chart in Figure 6.5. *High involvement* means just what it says. Your audience will get very involved with a buying decision. *Low involvement* is the opposite. The product is something your audience will buy, yet they don't really consider it seriously. *Think* means your best audience seriously considers this product or service. A tremendous amount of brain power and probably personal effort goes into this kind of buying decision. *Feel* indicates a high level of emotion accompanies the buying consideration.

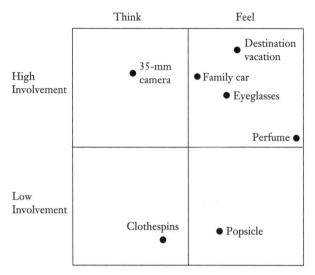

Figure 6.5 ▪ An Offer Chart from Foote Cone Belding (FCB Chart)

Let's look at an example using the FCB chart. A high involvement/think item is a 35-mm camera. If you are a camera buff or somebody in your family or one of your friends is seriously interested in photography, you understand. A while back I took a trip into the Himalayas. Since I enjoy photography, I took two cameras with me. We trekked at altitudes over 12,000 feet where our canteens of water froze solid every night. So did our cameras! Each morning, we had to wait until the sun came up in order to operate the cameras. The plastic inside the cameras became exceptionally brittle, the lubrication fluids seemed to freeze. The cameras were inoperable until the sun warmed them each morning. Shortly afterward, I spent 3 weeks sailing around Antarctica. Since my experience in the Himalayas had been frustrating, before the trip I went looking for a camera that wouldn't freeze in extremely cold weather. (In fact, I could not find a new camera that didn't have plastic in it. I had to buy a used one to get all metal parts.) You will undoubtedly agree that buying a camera is a very high involvement/think process.

A high involvement/feel process is getting a new pair of eyeglasses or contact lenses. If you wear glasses or contacts you will relate to this, particularly when your prescription changes or you get bifocals for the first time. There's lots of feel with glasses.

You may look at the FCB chart and not agree with the position of the dots. For example, I think the family car is much more a think item than it seems to indicate. Yes, emotion enters into the buying process for cars, but I personally would have put it in the think quadrant, close to the feel line.

Martin Gross, a direct marketing consultant and excellent copywriter, talks about high and low involvement. He gives it a media slant. In the language of marketing, direct mail and print are high involvement, while television and radio are low involvement. This has *nothing* to do with their effectiveness. Listening to the radio or watching television are passive activities. Reading mail or a print ad is an active process. Each can work when the message is of interest. What makes them effective is getting the right offer to the right audience at the right time. Boring is OUT; interesting is IN!

No matter, you need to look at your product or service and decide not only whether it is unique or not, if you are known or unknown, but also how your audience will look at it: high involvement, low involvement, think, or feel.

■ TIMELESS OFFER APPEALS ■

Brilliant marketer Jim Kobs pulled together a series of thoughts as to what people (and your audience is made up of people) need. Fulfilling that need with a sound offer will get you more orders. Here are some offers with timeless appeals:

■ People want to gain:

Health	Comfort
Popularity	Social advancement
Praise from others	Pride of accomplishment

Money   Self-confidence
Security in retirement   Time
Leisure   Appearance
Increased enjoyment   Personal prestige

- They want to:

Express their personalities   Satisfy their curiosity
Appreciate beauty   Win the affection of others
Resist domination by others   Emulate the admirable
Acquire or collect things   Improve themselves generally

- They want to save:

Time   Embarrassment
Discomfort   Work
Risks   Doubts
Money

- They want to be:

Good parents   Gregarious
Creative   "First" in things
Efficient   Sociable, hospitable
Recognized authorities   Proud of their possessions
Up-to-date   Influential over others

Where does your product fall under these four groupings?

- Gain
- Want to
- Save
- Want to be

Maybe it fits into more than one. Your offer will be affected by 1 or more of these factors. You, your position in your marketplace, and your product or service are each affected by how you are perceived and understood by your buyers.

■ Specialties, Premiums, and Your Offer ■

Direct response is a large user of advertising specialties and premiums. Here are just some of the ways they are put to use:

- To gain attention
- To build store or trade show traffic
- To inspire recall
- To promote an opening, anniversary, or other special event
- To activate inactive accounts
- To introduce a new product, name change, new reps, or a product enhancement
- To move products off the shelf
- To improve customer relations
- To simply say thank you

For the very reasons they are used for these and at least a score of other activities, they are important to consider when you plan your offer. Specialties and premiums get you attention. They get you consideration when it's time to buy.

Let's define an advertising specialty:

- It's a useful item for almost any purpose.
- It brings with it some message, usually as part of a totally integrated program, maybe carrying out the theme of the promotion.
- It comes with absolutely no strings attached; with no obligation.

A premium is a little different:

- It, too, is useful and usually of a higher value and quality.
- It carries a message, usually about a specific product or service promotion.

- It comes with a string attached. You must do something to earn the premium, maybe take a demonstration, take some positive action or step, possibly even make a buying decision. Premiums require action.

Direct response lead generation programs use both specialties and premiums. A specialty up front to get your attention, a premium on the back end when you make a buying decision.

Many traffic building programs offer a specialty for visiting the store or show booth. Mail-order marketers offer premiums for buying within a set time or for purchasing a minimum amount. Even fund-raisers have found premiums effective to increase donations.

Advertising Specialty and Premium Categories

There are 5 advertising specialty and premium categories. Every one of the over 25,000 items used as specialties or premiums falls into 1 of these categories.

Calendars

These include wall or desk, watch, wallet or purse, large, small, pop-up, monthly, quarterly, yearly or multiyear, multipage with beautiful pictures or artwork, or single page with a simple message. They are printed on paper, plastic, cloth, wood, film, and just about everything in between. Businesses use calendars in countless ways; the average home has four.

Writing Tools

These include pencils and pens of all types, shapes, sizes, styles, colors, and descriptions. They may come singly or in sets, by the dozen or gross, and in a wide variety of qualities and values, from a few pennies to hundreds of dollars. Some are premiums; some are specialties.

Business Gifts and Awards

These are usually upscale items worth a little more, things of "keep" value. They include functional desk sets and award/wall plaques. They may or may not carry the sponsor's name, logo, design, or other sales message. They are used as a reward, for goodwill, as a thank you, or as a gift for patronage.

Wearables

Clothing covers everything from head to toe, from hats and caps to dress shoes and sports socks, and almost everything in between. T-shirts and dress shirts, neckties and scarves, sports coats and team jackets, belts and belt buckles, sweaters, sweat suits and sweatbands—plus dozens of other ideas.

All Other Ideas

A wide variety of products fall in this catchall category, such as beer and coffee mugs, rulers, baggage tags, key chains, notebooks, luggage, briefcases, personal appearance items, and literally thousands of other ideas. All are used to meet an objective—to be remembered.

The Reason They Work: The R-10 Plan

Advertising specialties and premiums allow you to be in the marketplace on a continuing and ongoing basis. "Talking" with your audience frequently, sharing your message and the reason to do business together.

Reaching your target
audience with a **R**elevant message
Repeated again and again, over
and over, offering a **R**eward if they will
but **R**espond. If you are visible time
and time again, your **R**etention value goes up, and your
Recall value goes up.

Repetition
builds **R**eputation, and
you will be **R**emembered when it is time to buy.

When you can't be in front of your audience live or over the telephone, you are still there with an effective and useful specialty or premium. They remind your best customers and most "passionate" prospects you care and you want their business.

When you are planning your offer, give consideration to a specialty to begin and a premium to close. They make your offer just that much more powerful.

▪ THE GUARANTEE ▪

If you want to be the best, you have to separate yourself from all the talk about quality. And put it in writing.

Lee Iacocca

Every company guarantees its product or service, yet they don't all talk about it. I recommend you talk about it! In direct response, a discussion about your guarantee is almost imperative. It *is* imperative in mail order.

A guarantee of satisfaction certainly must be hinted at in all services offered. A guarantee can be implied as part of your offer, even when you're generating leads, raising funds, or building traffic through your store. Guarantees make people comfortable.

One of the things you don't want to do is have your attorney write a guarantee. It needs to be written by the marketing people. Make it simple, easy to understand, with short words. And speaking of short, maybe the best guarantee ever is from Lands' End. Figure 6.6 is a copy of their guarantee. Believe it? I sure do! And so do their customers.

Figure 6.6 ■ Lands' End Guarantee

The first written guarantee came from Benjamin Franklin:

Those persons who live remote, by sending their orders and money to said B. Franklin, may depend on the same justice as if present.

Benjamin Franklin had a store in Philadelphia. Many of the early settlers struck out across the Appalachians and into the midwestern plains. Franklin offered these people a mail-order service. He received their orders and shipped a variety of supplies and products. And he guaranteed his service even to "those persons who live remote."

Xerox learned that selling its fax equipment was as competitive as the copier marketplace. To be set apart from others, Xerox guarantees your fax message will arrive and backs it with the first and only (as far as I know) fax transmission guarantee:

If any fax you send on a new Xerox fax machine doesn't arrive in its entirety, we'll send you $5 for each undelivered document. No questions asked.

Here is the Baldwin Cooke Guarantee of Satisfaction or Your Money Back Offer:

If at any time you are not completely satisfied with your purchase, simply return it to Baldwin Cooke for replacement, or full and unconditional refund—including the cost of shipping both ways. Your satisfaction is our sole concern.

Here is a guarantee from a children's toy manufacturer, Judy Instructo:

> Our products are of the finest quality and the highest educational value. GUARANTEED. Return anything purchased from us that proves otherwise. We will replace the merchandise or refund your money as you wish.

Prime Time, a door-to-door airport shuttle service, offers this guarantee:

> We're on time or you don't pay.

That's a strong guarantee in a marketplace with heavy traffic such as southern California.

SGF guarantees your credit card won't be charged until your order is shipped. A strong guarantee from a mail-order marketer where credit card orders are a major source of its business.

The Company Store tells its mail-order buyers:

> If you don't hear a SMILE over the telephone, you've called the wrong number!

They "guarantee" you'll be happy with everything from The Company Store, including your phone conversation. To be doubly sure you're pleased, the telemarketer who takes your order includes a signed note with your shipment.

Another interesting guarantee comes from *American Demographics* magazine. They state their guarantee in the P.S. in their sales letter:

> Suppose disenchantment sets in later on? Still no problem. Then you can take us up on our explicit guarantee. Cancel

any time, for any reason, and we'll send you a full refund of your subscription price!

A most powerful and complete guarantee.

Lufthansa German Airlines introduced a guarantee program to its first and business class flyers. If the passengers (or their luggage) miss connecting flights and Lufthansa is at fault, the company pays the passengers $200.

Whirlpool offers a one-year product replacement guarantee. If for any reason the customer is not satisfied, they will replace your Whirlpool appliance with a new one. Both Whirlpool and Lufthansa are putting their wallets where their mouths are.

Seattle-based Nordstrom Department Stores has a customer satisfaction guarantee that is truly hard to beat. Although the story is an old one, it is worth repeating. A man stormed in to the service desk of a Nordstrom store, steaming mad. He demanded a refund on 2 automobile tires he claimed were defective. The store considered his request and on the spot wrote a check for the full value of the tires. The customer left a happy man. What makes this unusual? Nordstrom doesn't sell tires! They have no auto department, but this man was an important customer. And, since he thought he'd bought the tires at Nordstrom, who were they to argue? If they had pointed out that they didn't carry tires, the man would still have been mad, maybe embarrassed. By refunding the money, they kept a good customer happy.

Few of us can be as generous as Nordstrom. Yet all of us can guarantee our products and our service. All of us can make a "guarantee of customer satisfaction" offer. Quill, an office and computer supply mail-order house, includes a preauthorized return form with every guarantee of satisfaction shipment to make it easy for their customers to return any item for any reason. Spiegel, the major catalog house, offers free pick-up of merchandise customers may wish to return. The Lifetime Reconditioning Program guarantee of Shopsmith states the company will rebuild or replace its woodworking equipment at one third or less of the list price at the time of repair—a strong guarantee of satisfaction.

How about this for a guarantee? The initial public offering of common stock from Thermo Cardiosystems is guaranteed to increase in value. Guaranteed! And, if it doesn't? The company will buy it back for whatever the investors paid.

My favorite guarantee, seen in Sydney, Australia, on the back of a rubbish truck:

Satisfaction guaranteed or double your garbage back.

Nobody wants their garbage back. Yet, don't you believe this garbage man is the best in all of Sydney? His attitude is "I'm going to take care of my customers." He has a sense of humor about it and probably has a very large, satisfied customer base.

Another excellent guarantee comes from the mail-order Great Living people. They have the same super guarantee on their Web site as in their paper catalog.

SATISFACTION GUARANTEED . . . PERIOD! Our lifetime guarantee means just that! If, for ANY reason, a product you purchase from the Great Living catalog does not live up to your expectations (and it's strictly your decision!), we'll promptly replace the item or, if you prefer, issue a refund.

The 1980s brought us major industry deregulations. First in North America with airline freight services, soon followed by the passenger airlines. Next came long-haul trucking, telecommunications, and finance (which particularly affected banks).

In the 1990s, it began all over the world. Utilities are an example. All of a sudden, true competition was exploding in industries that had moved through the 20th century at their own speed. Lots of interesting things happened. Unfortunately, many firms went out of business. Why? Because they couldn't compete under the new rules. The good businesses prospered.

One of the good things happening in banking was a guarantee of service. The very thought of such a thing prior to deregulation was unthinkable. Guaranteed service—Wow, what a concept! It was truly revolutionary. Wells Fargo Bank started the trend by offering a 3-day service guarantee to all customers requesting a real estate loan. I don't know about where you live, but to get a yes or no answer on a home loan in 3 days was unheard of in my neighborhood. It was a great offer backed by a sound guarantee, which stated that for every day over 3 days it took Wells to get you an answer the bank would pay you $25. The idea has been picked up by others, all to the benefit of the consumer.

A guarantee is very important in direct response. Have one!

■ 10 Points to Remember About Offers ■

1. In traffic building programs and when generating leads, sell the offer, not your product or service. In mail order, you sell the product first with the offer as an extra benefit.
2. The closer your offer relates to your product or service, the higher the quality of your response.
3. The broader the appeal of your offer, the more action you will generate: money is universal (everybody uses it); cookbooks are almost universal; golf balls are limited.
4. Realize the importance of ego. Personalize your offer.
5. Your offer must be restated prominently on the order form or response device.
6. The more clearly you state the benefit of your offer, the higher the response.
7. Test offers only if your product or service will be the same the next time you make an offer.
8. The way you state your offer can be as important as the offer itself.
9. Make sure you have included all the true costs of your offer (product, handling, packaging, postage, etc.).
10. Know your audience *before* you select your offer.

▪ A Closing Word About Response Rates ▪

Almost without fail a question about response rates and what to expect comes up. How will your offer affect, change, or improve your response? What is often regarded as a typical or average response rate is around 2%. Please do not be misled by that number. It may, in fact, be typical for some subscription mailings, book offers, and catalog mailings. But response rates vary widely depending on the following factors:

- Medium (direct mail or space advertising, the Web, telephone or broadcast)
- Product (insurance versus recipe cards versus heavy-duty construction equipment)
- Offer (inquiry versus free trial versus cash with order versus booklet offer)
- Price ($39.95 versus $195 versus $2,000 versus $40,000 or more)
- List (customers or prospects)

There are other factors too, yet these are the main ones. Suffice it to say "normal" response can easily vary from 0.1% (that's 1/10 of 1%, which is not unusual in insurance or offers in print media) to 50% or more (yes, 50% is what happens when good direct mail or catalogs are mailed to long-established customers).

Your offer is next in importance to your audience. For you to be successful with *power direct marketing*, you need to take the time necessary to think about your offer. It will pay off.

Chapter 7

CREATIVE

It's Nice to Meet a Creative Person; All My Friends Are Serious

■ ■ ■

The creative process is the thing that gets us excited. It is also where we have the most opinions, where our biases and prejudices come quickly to the surface. The creative process is very subjective.

The direct response creative process, the sixth point of The 8ight Point Market Action Plan, cannot begin until the first 5 steps are in place:

- You know your objectives.
- A timetable has been set to achieve these objectives.
- A budget has been established to achieve your objectives within the time frame allowed.
- Your audience is clearly targeted and definitely reachable.
- You have some idea of what your offer should be.

Then, and ONLY then, can the creative process begin.

The purpose of creative is to maximize the impact of your message in order to increase the action from your marketplace. Maximize the impact and increase the action, remembering all along that "dull" is a 4-letter word. *Interesting* is what your creative must be.

When it is, you are well on your way to success with power direct marketing.

■ The Creative Planning Process—a Checklist ■

The purpose of the creative process is to take you to profitable marketing objectives. The checklist in this section contains the tactics (the *do* part of planning) needed to help you do just that—reach your objectives. This assumes you have spelled out your goals with a clear focus. If you have not and your presentation is a foggy nonmessage, your audience will know.

To help you avoid this situation, I've created this list. The original concept came from a book by Joe Reynolds called *Out Front Leadership*. I liked his base strategy learned over 30 years at Procter & Gamble and adapted it to direct marketing creative.

My 22 thoughts raise the traditional *how, what, where, who, why,* and *when* questions. You may not need to answer each question; you *do* need to look at each and ask

- How am I going to reach our objectives within the allocated time frame and allowed budget?
- What do I need to do now and in the future to reach our goals?
- Where are we headed, and how can the creative process get us there?
- Who is our marketplace, and what are all the ways to reach these people?
- Why does anyone want to buy the products we sell and services we offer?
- When is our market ready to buy, and when are our sales reps ready to sell?

After you've addressed and answered these 6 broad queries, you are ready to be creative with the 22 Creative Planning Process questions:

1. **What is the base idea?** Meaning the rock-bottom creative idea. What are you trying to do, to achieve, to make happen?

2. **Is this a good idea?** Or is this idea only "creative"? Is it built on a long-term idea, or is it just promotional?

3. **If this is a good idea, WHY is it so good?** What does it do or offer toward achieving your objectives with your customers and with your prospects (2 very different audiences)?

4. **How does this idea mesh with your already stated and understood company values?** Does it walk in the same direction you are headed, on track? Or is it off the road?

5. **What about your mission, your vision, your purpose?** Does this creative idea complement or compete with those standards? What about with your focus, your direction, your position, your image in the marketplace?

6. **What is the potential for this idea with those who buy what you sell?** How large an idea is it? Does it cover your total audience? How much universal appeal will it actually have? What can you expect to happen with this creative idea?

7. **Has anyone else in your industry tried this creative idea before?** If so, who? And what happened—are they still using it? If so, should you? If so, what are the expected results? If not, why not?

8. **What about this idea in other industries?** Has it been tried elsewhere? By looking outside your direct marketplace, do you see others doing what you want to do? If so, who are these people? What level of success are they enjoying?

9. **If this idea has been tried by others, when did that happen?** At that time, what else was happening in the marketplace to affect success?

10. **Why was this idea a success . . . or not?** Simply, yes or no, did it work? Short-term? Or long-term? Both?

11. **What resources are needed to make this idea happen the right way?** How about people? Time? Money? Systems? Other support? Even good ideas do not just happen; they demand support to be successful. Do you have access to all needed resources?

12. **Should you choose to run with this idea, when will these resources need to be committed?** In other words, what is the timetable to get everything in place? Usually everything is not needed at the same time, yet there still needs to be a schedule. Do you have such a schedule?

13. **What is the process to mesh people with the idea?** With the systems? With the immediate objectives? With the overall task? With what is to be achieved? Who does what, and when?

14. **Who needs to be in control?** Who is in charge? What person holds power over the creative decisions to be made? Where does the buck stop?

15. **What do the people who are making all this happen think of the creative idea?** Do they like it or not? Are they committed to it? What about the sales team and management? Is everyone fully committed?

16. **What are all the ways you can communicate this idea to your marketplace?** To gain the maximum response and positive results, what media will you need?
    - Direct mail marketing
    - Direct response print
    - Direct response broadcast
    - Merchandising
    - Public relations
    - Sales promotion
    - The World Wide Web
    - Any and all other means and methods

17. **What about frequency?** How often will you communicate with your marketplace? It is mandatory to consider this often overlooked part of the creative process up front. Have you?

18. **What is the timetable for your communication plan to come to market?** Combined with the media use and frequency question, what will your *realistic* schedule be?

19. **What is the financial plan for this creative idea?** Do you have sufficient funds to make it happen? Whether a Salvation Army or Rolex budget—do you have the resources you need?

20. **Have you thought about the "what-if" plus and "what-if" minus situations?** The SWOT (Strengths, Weaknesses, Opportunities, Threats) analysis applies here. Have you evaluated every aspect of "what-if"?

21. **How are you going to measure the results?** What is your creative plan to complete the circle, to tie the creative process to back-end results? Be certain to decide *before* going to market what it takes to be successful in the marketplace. Have you done so?

22. **Now, how soon do you begin?** When do you begin this creative process? A portion of this plan is to think DIRFT (Do It Right the First Time). Although this may be an unlikely happening, it is still part of being ready. Do you have the DIRFT philosophy?

Power direct marketing works when you engage the brain before the fingers. When you ask—and answer!—before doing. The Creative Planning Process gets you headed in that direction.

■ CREATIVE QUESTIONS TO CONSIDER ■

Okay, now what? You've addressed the corporate issue and are ready to roll. What's next? The purpose of the creative process is to generate a

breakthrough message and to communicate that message with benefits of the product or service to your target audience.

Sometimes we forget this important principle in marketing, direct
marketing, and direct response advertising: *The objective of marketing is
to determine what your audience needs and provide that service or product.*

Here is a collection of creative questions to consider as you
begin to plan your copy and art—to make 110% certain you ARE
reaching your audience with a message they want to receive.

1. How are your product positioning, product features,
   and their related benefits best stated?
   - How are they different from those of your
     competition?
2. Are buying-decision incentives desired or needed?
   - How do you present them to motivate?
   - How do you present them to gain a call to action?
   - What do you use?
   - When do you use it?
3. What methods should be used to offer your product?
   What approach?
   - A 1-, 2-, or 3-step approach?
4. What media mix should you use?
   - Direct mail?
   - Space?
   - Telephone?
   - Broadcast?
   - Collateral?
   - World Wide Web?
   - Other?
5. What do you need for:
   - Traffic building?
   - Lead generation?
   - Mail order?
   - Fund-raising?

6. How do you motivate to action based on quantitative information?

■ MEASURABLE RESULTS ■

Direct marketing is tied to selling. And, since selling is getting your prospect to make a buying decision to purchase from you, direct marketing and selling work together.

The direct response creative team has the responsibility to prepare the message to achieve the objectives, to get results. There is no other measure! Only results matter, as you can see in Figure 7.1.

When you care enough to know what is really happening in your marketplace, when you want to know what part of your marketing program is working, you use direct response. You go for and get measurable results.

Direct marketing is *ACTION*-oriented. Your prospect is supposed to do something, take some action toward the buying process. Redeem the coupon. Call the toll-free number. Make a donation. Come into the store. Visit the trade show booth. Fill in and mail the order form. Reply through your Web site. DO SOMETHING!

Direct marketing is *MEASURABLE*. You can count what happens. How many customers come in your door, mail in the coupon, call in an order or order via e-mail, buy the product—DO SOMETHING.

Finally, direct marketing gains the SALE! It is either the sale itself as in mail order and fund-raising, or it leads to the sale as in traffic building and lead generation.

There are 4 major components for creating a successful direct response mail package, catalog, print advertisement, or Web site:

- Headline or teaser copy
- Copy
- Graphics
- Response

RESULTS	*Results* are what you want.
MEASURABLE RESULTS!	Results are useful only if they are measurable. Your program must be designed to get you measurable results.
FEATURES	FEATURES come first, the red button or fancy handle.
NEEDS Features	NEEDS for those features must be explained to suspects. Why they can hardly live without them.
ADVANTAGES Needs Features	The ADVANTAGES of how you can put these features to work for customers must be explained next.
BENEFITS Advantages Needs Features	The BENEFITS, the "results" to customers, is the next step up the ladder. What happens when they push the red button or turn the fancy handle?
SALES POINTS Benefits Advantages Needs Features	All must be expressed as SALES POINTS, presented in a way that allows you to "Ask for the Order!"
MEASURABLE RESULTS Sales points Benefits Advantages Needs Features	And only then will you have MEASURABLE RESULTS.

Figure 7.1 ▪ Measurable Results Ladder

▪ Getting Started with Creative by the Numbers: A List of 99 Creative Ideas ▪

This section is a collection of how-to guidelines. Ideas to help you develop good direct response mail-order packages and catalogs, traffic building and lead generation programs.

1. Before putting pen to paper, know as much as you can about your audience.

Put yourself in the place of the person to whom you're writing. What are the outstanding benefits of your product or service? What are the primary needs of your prospect? How do these benefits and needs mesh together? What would make *you* buy? Write to that viewpoint.

2. Before putting pen to paper, know as much as you can about your product.

Research your product until you find its unique benefit, the one your competition can't or won't match. The one big benefit (sometimes there are 2 or even 3—rarely more) of your product is what will make people buy. It's also what you should build your story around. Find that benefit, then run wild with it.

Keep It Short and Simple

KISS (Keep It Short and Simple) as a philosophy works best in direct response. Here are a few ideas that follow that thinking.

3. Make your message as easy to understand as possible.

The apostle Paul knew the importance of being simple and clear. He said:

> Except ye utter by the tongue words easy to understand, how shall it be known what is spoken? For ye shall speak into the air.

Keep your words, sentences, and paragraphs short. Stay away from the long and complicated. A good rule to follow: For every 100 words you write, double-check to make sure 70 of those 100 words are 5 letters or less.

4. How long should a sentence be? SHORT!

Dr. George R. Klare of Ohio University reports research that rates ease of reading for copy as follows:

Level	Sentence Length
Very easy to read	8 words
Easy	11 words
Fairly easy	14 words
Standard	17 words
Fairly difficult	21 words
Difficult	25 words
Very difficult	Over 29 words

Sentences should be short with only one idea to a sentence. A good rule of thumb is to keep sentences to an average of 14 words or 25 syllables—OR LESS. In all of Hemingway's writings, his sentence length ranged from 1 to 49 words with an average of 13.5. Write like Hemingway!

Remember Western Union telegrams that said "stop" after each brief sentence? Try it with your writing. Simply put a period—a stop—in more often. It works.

If you follow this guideline, you'll be read more, because you will have made your copy easy to read.

5. Paragraphs should be short, with no more than 7 lines of copy before you break for a new paragraph.

There is no rule that says the same thought can't carry over into 2, 3, or more paragraphs. Limit your paragraphs to 7 lines. (Please note the word is "lines," NOT "sentences!") It will make your copy easier to read.

6. Words should be short. Five-letter words are readable.

Yes, you must use the language of your market. If that audience is highly educated or has much technical knowledge, they may expect you to be their equal. So, talk to them in their language.

That does not mean your copy should become difficult to read. Your audience, no matter their level of expertise, is still made up of people. The easier your words are to read, the more likely they will understand your message and respond to your offer.

Use lots of 1-, 2-, 3-, 4-, and 5-letter words. Short words work.

7. Use familiar words.

Avoid difficult words. Your copy must be familiar to your audience.

If you are introducing a new concept, keep your explanation simple. Couch your appeal in the language of the customer. Doctors don't respond to the same appeal as plumbers, teenagers as grandparents. From mountain climbers to beach bums, they are all different audiences. Use the words of the people you are trying to reach.

Facts Are Stubborn Things

Facts are believable, whereas general statements are generic. Using FACTS in your creative will make you more believable and gain you a better response.

8. Give your copy news value.

> *It takes hard writing to make easy reading.*
> Robert Louis Stevenson

Use facts, use names, and be specific. Tell who, what, why, when, where, and how.

9. Copy that sells is copy that is long on hard facts and benefits.

Copy is not short. Copy is not long. Copy is interesting or uninteresting. It is really as simple as that.

If the copy is interesting to your readers, your marketplace, they will read it—or at least review it. And there is a good chance they will take some action. If the copy fails the "interesting" test, nothing will happen.

10. Be as exact as possible.

The number 481 is much more believable than "almost 500." $16.42 is more believable than the retail price of $14.95. It is not always easy to be exact with your information; when you can be, your message is more likely to be understood and acted on.

Here are some very specific and some generic numbers:

Specific	Generic
60 seconds	1 minute
60 minutes	1 hour
24 hours	1 day
30 days	1 month
12 months	1 year
365 days	1 year

Here are several more specific examples.

Last year, attendance at harness racing tracks totaled 26 million people. They wagered just under $5.2 billion on 57,000 horses, which raced for $511 million.

YKK accounts for 51% of the world's zipper supply. The company churns out 1.1 million miles of zippers annually—enough to circle the earth 44 times!

Over a period of 12 months, according to a report from Nielsen Clearing House, 215.6 billion money-saving grocery product coupons were distributed in America. Consumers redeemed 7.15 billion of them, saving nearly 40¢ each time, or over $2.84 billion total.

11. Facts about product benefits are more powerful than claims. Use:

- Case histories
- Statistics
- Performance figures
- Names
- Dates
- Quotes from experts
- Any facts you can find

Facts, such as color, size, shape, weight, length, height, and width, should all be specific. You'll find your copy becomes more believable and more successful.

12. Testimonial copy provides some of the most effective written words for any offer—business or consumer, any product or service.

Get testimonials from your clients. Then use them in your direct mail, your space ads, on your Web site, and in your catalogs. Everywhere.

The most believable testimonials include the quote and the person's picture, name, title, company, and city. Anything less than this begins to compromise the testimonial's credibility. This doesn't mean using it is not a good idea if, for instance, a picture is not available. Just that something is lost.

13. Ditto for case history stories.

"Live" examples from real situations allow your copy to paint a complete picture, to tell the entire story. Dig in your files and find examples of superior service, outstanding success with amazing results. Tell your prospects what your product or service will do.

14. Know the difference between a product feature ***and a product*** benefit, ***and keep them separate.***

A feature

- helps to distinguish one product from another;
- is a characteristic of the product or service you are selling; and
- is inherent in the product—it is part of the product, whether or not it is sold.

A benefit

- ties the product feature to the customer's NEEDS;
- is the good the buyer gains from your product/service; and
- *cannot* exist without a buyer.

Your readers are less interested in what your product *is* than what it will *do*. So, fill your letter and response device with all the ways your product will help the reader make money, have fun, save time, improve life. Remember, people do not buy red buttons; they buy what happens when they push red buttons. A feature is a quarter-inch drill; the benefit is the quarter-inch hole. A feature is a safety lock; the benefit is the security you feel when you use the lock.

Save the necessary but less exciting technical stuff for the brochure or flyer. Sell with benefits.

15. Sell the sizzle, not the steak.

An original saying from sales pro Elmer Wheeler, this rule dates back to the golden days of salesmanship. It's a basic. And an essential rule to remember when putting your sales points on paper.

What it means, quite simply, is to discover the reason why your customer will want to buy your product. Sell the excitement, the benefit, the peace of mind, the satisfaction your product offers.

Sell the sizzle, not the steak.

16. Here are 6 key words that will aid you in writing.

Before your first draft:

- Think
- Plan
- Organize

After the first draft:

- Revise
- Revise
- REVISE!

Just as you revise important interoffice memos going up the ladder, revise your direct response copy, too. You want your audience to get your best effort.

Headlines and Other Beginnings

17. Consider the following ideas when writing your headlines and your teaser copy.

- Does the copy relate to the offer?
- Does it offer a benefit?
- Does it urge action?
- Does it tie to the opening of the letter or the first paragraph in the advertisement?
- Do the graphics and the copy tie together?
- Does it avoid imitation?
- Does it have a "YOU" attitude?
- Does it "talk with" the reader?

18. If you don't get your reader to open your mail package none of the "rules" will do you any good.

Okay, so how do you do it? There are basically 4 schools of thought:

- Whet your prospects' appetite by promising a benefit or making an intriguing statement about what they will learn. Tease your readers (hence the term "teaser copy").
- Use a dramatic graphic design. We live in a very visual era when strong, bold, interesting, different graphics draw attention.
- State your offer loud and clear. No kidding—be blunt with your approach.
- Use a blank envelope to create curiosity. This idea can work, especially if your company is very well known, or if the person to whom you are mailing is a customer, or you're mailing to top-level executives.

19. Your teaser and your headline copy should do one or more of the following things.

- *Explain* who you are, what the offer is, and what the benefits will be.

- *Entertain* your prospects with something just a tick humorous. This is the teaser part to get them inside the envelope or to read your ad (be very careful with humor, it can backfire).
- *Enhance* the product or service you are offering. This works best when you are upgrading or cross-selling a product to your own customer base.

20. Solid, information-packed headlines usually work.

And they work better than cute, double-meaning phrases. Good headline words include:

- Find out
- Send for
- Learn
- Buy

21. In direct mail, the opening paragraph of a letter should not exceed 11 words.

In space advertising, the headline should follow that same general rule: keep it to 11 words. It will get read, because it is easier to read.

There is a second opinion on headlines. Some marketers feel they can go to 17 words without losing readership. Maybe! My suggestion is still short.

22. The headline that carries the name of your product or company or both can more directly target your audience.

Five times as many people will read the headline as will read the ad. So, get your name up front and tell your readership what you want them to know.

23. Don't stop with your first headline or your 10th or your 50th. Keep rewriting. Keep revising, improving.

A suggestion from David Ogilvy: start with a sheet of paper numbered from 1 to 100 and don't stop revising until you hit 100. The longer you work at it, the more effective your headlines will be.

24. *Here are a few words that work well for both headlines and teaser copy.*

Compare	More	Easy
Price	Introduce	New
Now	Save	

And, that ever popular word, FREE.

25. *Don't stop with your first copy draft, either.*

We're talking hard work. Still, the experts don't always follow the same rules.

> *An ad is not an intellectual exercise, and the longer you take to write it, the further away you get from the person you're talking to.*
>
> Reva Korda
Creative Head
Ogilvy & Mather

> *The person hasn't been born yet who can sit down and dash off a great piece of direct mail copy. It is hard work. There are no short-cuts. Almost without exception, the success of any direct mail letter is in direct ratio to the time spent on its preparation.*
>
> Bob Stone
Chairman of the Board
Stone & Adler

Two points of view from 2 experts. You choose. Put the top 25 direct marketing writers in a room and take a vote. (I've got my money on the Bob Stone point of view!)

26. *Write better with MADE.*

M 5 Message (Give a message to your audience.)

A 5 Action (Have a reason for taking action now.)

D 5 Details (Provide enough details so your audience can make a buying decision.)

E 5 Evidence (Prove what you have to offer will meet the needs of your marketplace. Provide the evidence.)

27. Dazzle them with a string of pearls.

Your headline is the place to hook readers with one dominant benefit. But once they are reading, pile on all the secondary benefits. All to increase their appetite for your product.

Take readers from one strong benefit to another, all the way through your clincher copy. Put the strongest benefits at the beginning and keep one big one for last, especially if it's unexpected or unusual.

28. Get to your main point, your BIG benefits, and do it quickly.

This is an important point for copywriters, copy chiefs, and creative directors. It's not uncommon to take too long to get to the main point and the benefits to the reader.

Frequently, you'll find you can cut 1, 2, or 3 paragraphs from the beginning of a letter, thus allowing it to move quickly. You can count on being more effective when you do so.

29. Joe Sugarman of JS&A products, one of the world's most successful copywriters, says, "The purpose of every element in an advertising headline, subhead, or illustration is to get your reader to read the first sentence."

Your opening statement has to be dramatic. Use nonintimidating first sentences of 3, 4, or 5 words. Sugarman calls it "greased chute copy"—pull 'em in on the first sentence and they'll slide down to the last.

Letters

30. Always include a letter to personalize your copy.

One of direct mail's biggest advantages over mass media is its ability to make personal one-to-one contact. So, don't blow it by leaving out the most personal part of your package—the letter.

A letter doesn't need to be long or fancy; still, direct mail does need some kind of letter. Many marketers include a simulated letter inside their catalog as part of a self-mailer. Why? Because it makes direct mail more personal.

31. *The letter is the most important element in a direct mail or mail-order package.*

Research shows 65% of your response will come because of the copy in the letter. So, it is very important to be selective in your salutation. Stay away from the trite and stuffy "standard" openings. Instead, be friendly and personal.

Use a name if available. If not, relate your salutation to the audience. Here are a few examples:

Dear Tennis Nut,
Dear Marketing Executive,
Dear World Traveler,
Dear Collector,
To the Person in Charge of _____,

Try it, it works!

32. *Write to people, not companies.*

People make decisions, companies don't. People are the actors in daily life; they create the drama of the office, factory, and home. In every organization.

Your copy should call these people out by name if possible and by title without fail:

Engineer
Accountant
Sales representative
Mother
Supervisor
Home owner
Plumber
Grandfather

President
Member
Executive secretary
Receptionist
Swimmer
Photographer
Or whatever . . .

Write to people 1-on-1.

33. Spacing of copy is very important.

In all the elements of your direct mail, print advertising, your catalog, everywhere. Single space paragraphs; double space between
paragraphs.

34. A printed letter looks more personal when you use the following.

- An exact date
- A salutation
- Indented paragraphs
- Short paragraphs
- A complimentary close and signature
- A P.S.

Compromise by removing any of these elements and your letter will start becoming an institutional blurb instead of a personal
communication. As copy pro and direct marketing guru Bob
Hemmings says, "The best direct mail is a letter to mother . . .
multiplied."

Write personal direct mail.

35. Always use typewriter-style type for your letters.

Never typeset them. It takes away from the personal feeling of your
letter. Even with fancy desktop publishing and word processing,

typewriter-type letters still look more personal. Use Courier, Garamond, and Times Roman styles.

36. Here are my 8 golden guidelines on how to write a direct response sales letter.

- The best way is the simple way. WRITE IT LIKE YOU SAY IT! Don't concern yourself with punctuation (we overuse it anyway). Don't wordsmith every sentence. Make it human.

We all use simple words when we talk. (How many of us really understand Bill Buckley?) Use these same 1- and 2-syllable words when you write. Write it like you'd say it.

- The best mail is personal mail multiplied. Write to your Aunt Minnie (or, if you don't like Auntie M, your favorite somebody). And do it over and over and over to others. It works.

- If your audience is octogenarians in Oshkosh, then you become an octogenarian in Oshkosh. Pretend you are the recipient and write to yourself. Presidents of large companies respond differently from those of smaller firms, women from men, musicians from architects. Write to your audience, talk to them with whatever common denominator is available. Put yourself in your reader's frame of mind.

- Never, but NEVER, talk down to your audience. Look them straight in the eye, aim at them directly. Or even better, look up to them.

- Do not tell a lie. Be honest, straightforward, up front, truthful. Tell a funny story, be entertaining, weave a theme to make your point, play games any way that will help your cause. Do not tell a lie—ever. Period!

- Have something to say. This may seem funny to have to point out, yet many letters don't say anything. Have something specific to say, a message, and then say it. Don't beat around the bush—come out with it.

- Make an offer. The offer says if readers do this now, these good things will happen to them now. Respond in 30 days and get a free thingamajig. Save 10%. Win a bonus gift or a choice of . . . The offer is the reason a certain percentage of your audience will respond, and it many times is the difference between success or failure. Move those "considering" you to your side with a good offer.

■ ASK FOR THE ORDER! Be specific; ask your audience to do something. Come into your store with the coupon, mail back the card for the free booklet, call you for an appointment, make a donation, send for the product, order the service—whatever it is, ask for the order.

Don't just hint. Spell it out in spades. What do you want me, the audience, to do? Tell me what to do, the benefits of doing it, the benefits of doing it now. Make your offer clear. No matter how you do it, AFTO.

More About Copy

37. *Don't be a slave to grammar.*

Use "thought units" when you write. Copywriting and English composition are two different things. Feel free to ignore the grammarians' rules if they get in the way of clear, forceful communication. (Your 9th-grade English teacher isn't around to give you an F anymore.)

This doesn't mean you should write like an illiterate! If your copy's tone and rhythm call for them, go ahead and use sentence fragments. And run-ons. And split infinitives. Be conversational!

You don't worry about grammatical technicalities when you do face-to-face selling. Why get uptight when you write direct mail or a response ad?

38. *Make your copy inviting.*

All it takes is a felt pen, a photo or 2, and a little imagination. As a rule, people do not read direct mail to be entertained.

Long copy blocks are foreboding. Break up your copy with:

■ Subheads
■ Color
■ /Slashes/
■ Bullets (•)

- Asterisks (*)
- <u>Underlining</u>
- (Parentheses)
- CAPPED words

Use these graphic devices sparingly or you'll lose the emphasis you're trying to achieve.

39. *Prospects read more of your letter if you make it hard for them to stop at the end of the page.*

End the page in mid-sentence or even mid-word and put in "Please turn," "over," or "More benefits on the other side." Use graphic devices such as a handdrawn arrow pointing right.

Don't give your readers a place to take a breather or they may take a walk instead.

40. *Use active sentences and phrases.*

Watch yourself so you don't write things like, "Your car's performance is improved 4 ways by Widget Additive" when you should say, "Widget Additive improves your car's performance 4 ways."

For most writing, you'll benefit by staying in the active voice. You'll save words and make it more inviting for your reader to stay with you.

41. *Make your copy dramatic.*

State a specific benefit. Make it so enticing your reader will have to read on. Use words, phrases, thoughts, and ideas that paint a picture, tell a story, get your reader involved. Remember, you are looking for ACTION. Encourage him or her to take some.

42. *Dick Benson said: "The longer you can keep someone reading your copy, the better your chance of selling them."*

Readership studies show you have the first 50 words in a direct mail letter, a print ad, or a brochure to grab your audience. When you get them to read 50, there is every reason to believe they'll read 500. If they don't . . .

43. From many sources and countless "live" examples in the marketplace, come the 13 Magic Words of direct response.

Can you name them?

- Free
- Save
- Now
- Revolutionary
- Breakthrough

- Today
- You
- Yes
- Easy
- Introducing

- New
- Guarantee
- Win

What you see here are the most effective, proven, and tested magic words in direct response.

44. David Ogilvy says the following words and phrases also work wonders.

- How to . . .
- Suddenly
- Announcing
- Improved
- Miracle
- Magic

- Amazing
- Sensational
- Remarkable bargain
- Advice to . . .
- The truth about . . .
- Quick

- Last chance
- Hurry
- It's here!
- Just arrived

Try 'em!

45. If you're friendly in your copy, you'll make friends for your product and company.

Show your reader there's a warm, honest, flesh-and-blood human being on the other end of that number, order form, Web site, reply envelope, or coupon. Your customers appreciate old-fashioned friendliness, just as you do.

46. Make your copy as long as it needs to be.

You may want to tease and not give all the facts about the product. But make your copy long enough to tell your story, then quit. No copy is too long if it holds the reader's interest. One sentence is too long if it doesn't. Long copy will outpull short copy if everything you say is interesting.

The *Direct Response Marketing to Schools Newsletter* reports longer usually outpulls shorter for direct mail sales letters. A 2-page letter will usually pull about 80% more than 1 page. A 4-page sales letter generally pulls 50% more than 2 pages. (Please note: these are "averages"—and none of us are average!)

An exception may be lead generation letters. Keep in mind busy executives may feel they don't have time to read a long message. And no one has time to read anything they are not interested in.

47. Generally speaking, attempts at humor in direct mail fail.

Like any of the "rules" here, there can be exceptions. Humor can be a great attention getter. For some products, if used well, humor can be used throughout a package to entertain and to get orders. Sometimes a little humor will work when tied to a theme, a special limited time offer, something timely.

As with most direct response rules, test carefully up front before rolling out a humorous or any such campaign.

48. The more you tell, the more you sell.

There is no such thing as too much copy. Remember, "Nobody reads the white space."

The United States Postal Service found from a study that "64% of the households don't really mind an influx of direct mail packages as long as they are interesting." Similar results are reported by Schlenker Research Services about outbound telemarketing. Overall, 38% of consumers "don't really mind" receiving a telemarketing call. And the number gets higher—47%—with calls to those under 35 years of age.

Make your message interesting and say all there is to say. Never mail blank pages. Use all the space available in a magazine or newspaper. Keep your catalog full. Say or write enough to get the lead or to get the order. Whatever it takes, do it.

49. Words are important.

Here are some big things with little names:

- Life and death
- Peace and war

- Day and night
- Smile, cry, and laugh
- Faith and hope
- Love and hate

50. Direct mail great Ed Mayer included on his list of important words some with grace, charm, and impact:

- Lull, purr, and muck
- Drench and parch
- Nip, twang, sweet, tart, wet, and dry
- Force, speed, and slow
- Blast and boom
- Throb and thump
- Chime, hiss, buzz, and zoom

These are powerful words. Use them where they fit.

51. Maxwell Ross prepared a list of sentences he calls the "Bucket Brigade."

Here are some of them. These are phrases that take you from where you are (the offer) to the next step in getting your audience to take action:

- "But, that's not all."
- "And now you can . . ."
- "So, that is why . . ."
- "Or, if you prefer . . ."
- "Now—here is all you do."
- "Better yet . . ."
- "More important than that . . ."
- "And in addition to that . . ."

52. More "Bucket Brigade" IDEAS:

- "When you first . . ."
- "Let me show you how . . ."
- "Within the next few days . . ."

- "You may wonder why . . ."
- "Here is the reason why . . ."
- "As you probably know . . ."
- "Now, here is the next step."
- "So, you'll be glad to know . . ."

53. Stay away from me-me copy. Make your copy a dialogue, not a monologue.

Copywriting is communication, and that takes 2. If your copy is filled with "I," "we," and "our company," don't be surprised if the reader ignores you. Instead, concentrate on what the product or service does for the reader.

Many successful packages use "you" to begin as many as *half* the paragraphs. Mention yourself, to be sure. Yet talk to the "you" who's waiting to hear what you'll do for them.

54. Give your copy to someone else to read.

The first time they read it, did they get the emphasis you wanted? Did they understand it the first time? If so, fine. If not, it is back to the keyboard.

Remember, in direct response, direct mail, space ads, catalogs, and still today on the Web —IT IS COPY THAT SELLS! Copy is king. If your words are not understood, no amount of superb graphics can save your package or make your offer work.

55. Be a copycat.

Every direct response copywriter and art director need a "SWIPE" file. If you don't have one, make one. This is probably your best indicator as to what is happening in direct response. SWIPE means just what it says, steal ideas from others. No one has a lock on good ideas. If you see something someone else did and can use it for yourself, do it!

56. Keep up-to-date on what's happening in direct marketing.

Where your schedule, budget, and quantity allow, experiment with the latest printing techniques. Familiarize yourself with new, different, and unusual printing processes. With plastic envelopes, zipvelope mailings, and gold foil stamping.

Learn about 3-dimensional mailing options. Did YOU ever get a 3-D or lumpy package, a box or tube, anything "odd" in shape or size or even color you didn't open? No! Ditto for your prospect and customers.

Join your industry trade organization. Ask your suppliers to make a presentation to your creative staff. Have lunch with your printers.

Read *Direct Marketing, Target Marketing, DM News, Direct, Catalog Age, Direct Marketing International,* and whatever newsletters and specialty publications address your special needs.

Getting a Response, Making an Offer

57. A money-back or satisfaction guarantee is worth its weight in gold to a direct marketer.

It's a powerful tool for overcoming suspicion. The stronger you can make it, the more it will increase your response.

Do you know any company that doesn't guarantee its product or service? Everyone I deal with does, or I don't deal with them! So, since you want happy and satisfied customers, offer a guarantee.

Or, as Ray Considine says: DWYPYWD—Do what you promised you would do.

58. Besides telling the positive reasons for responding to your message, a guarantee helps point out what the reader will lose by not responding.

Sometimes what they feel they're going to lose moves people to action more than what they might gain. Such as the opportunity to buy at a low introductory price; the chance to buy, period, if the supply is limited; the bigger profits, improved health, greater beauty, or whatever your product or service offers.

59. Premiums work!

If the customer doesn't have to send money with the order, this can be an irresistible offer.

The more closely your premium relates to your product, the better it will be. (In most cases. There is a theory that your premium should have nothing to do with your offer, so your prospect doesn't mix things up. I subscribe to the related concept.)

You select your premium from thousands on the market or you create one. For example, if your product is a book, consider offering an excerpt from that book or a similar book.

60. *Make it easy for your prospect to order your product; make it easy to respond to your appeal.*

- Offer a booklet or sample.
- Offer a free trial.
- Offer a free cost estimate.
- Offer an easy payment plan.
- Explain in explicit terms how to order and then make ordering as simple as possible.
- Use a coupon, order form, or reply card.
- Include 2 or more reply forms.

61. *It's vital to get your reader involved emotionally in the benefits of what you're offering.*

If you can get your prospect physically involved in your mailing piece, you've got a big edge. You do this by designing in an "involvement device" such as one of the following:

- A peel-off token from the letter to stick on the reply card
- A scratch 'n' sniff area
- A pop-up
- Anything you have to punch out
- A sample of the product or material
- A component that unfolds in an interesting way
- An intriguing gimmick or advertising specialty
- A rub-off/scratch-off spot
- A printed or die-cut measuring device
- A simple puzzle
- A connect-the-dots activity

You will get extra mileage by showing your product through a window of the envelope. Or at least writing teaser copy about it on the envelope.

While it's true that making it easy to respond generally increases your response, it's also true that giving the customer an interesting, enjoyable, or challenging task can boost response as well.

The things in our list work because they appeal to the child in each of us.

62. Remember the 6 PRoductivity Building Blocks, compliments of Tom Collins.

- PRoduct. What's unique? What's the Unique Selling Proposition (USP) of your service?
- PRospect. Who is your audience; who needs this product or service?
- PRoblem. Why is what you offer going to meet a need, and what need will it meet?
- PRomise. What will your product do for the marketplace; what is its application?
- PRoof. Why should anyone believe you; what is your guarantee? Do you share a case history? What about testimonials?
- PRoposition. What is your deal, your offer? Why should the market respond? And why now?

63. The lift letter, also known as a publisher's letter, pub letter, or president's letter, will almost always increase your response.

The lift letter is the letter that says: "Please read this if you've decided not to buy." A lift letter is usually shorter and smaller (printed on a smaller piece of paper) than the main letter. The lift letter works very well in mail order, fund-raising, and sometimes lead generation.

Consider putting one in every package or testing with and without one, especially to consumer audiences.

64. *No direct response ad, mail package, or catalog is complete without a call to action, a response device.*

Preferably more than one! Do not assume your customers or prospects know what you want them to do. Tell them! Tell your marketplace to call a toll-free number, place an order, clip the coupon, fill out the business response card and mail it, bring the ticket to your store, visit your trade show booth, send money.

Whatever it is you want in the way of action, make sure your message is clear.

65. *Tell your audience more than once what to do; REPEAT the message.*

McGraw-Hill says to repeat your offer 7 times. Which means repeat your offer and encourage your reader to accept your offer over and over. Several times in your mail package and print ad, on television and at your Web site. In the P.S. to your letter, brochure, flyer, testimonial insert. Obviously on the order form or response card. Tell your readers again and again you want to do business with them.

66. *The less the commitment, the more likely the response.*

In your direct mail packages, always consider options such as "bill me," credit cards, and installment orders, as well as offering a toll-free phone or fax number and e-mail.

Regarding "bill me" payments: the increase in the number of orders many times makes up for the increase in bad debts. However, make certain someone is keeping tabs on bad debts.

67. *Limited time offers work; try them.*

"Good for only 30 days" will increase your action NOW, when you want it. Use a specific date. "Good only until April 10" lets your audience know they have a limited time to take advantage of this special opportunity. Limited time offers work. Try 'em.

68. The most important sentences in direct mail are the first and last. Your P.S. is one of the best read parts of a direct mail letter. Use one.

Use one in every letter you write. Make certain it contains important information—an important benefit or some other piece of information you want to repeat to your reader. It must suggest your thinking, or suggest buying, or tell the reader what to do, and say when and how to do it!

69. If 1 P.S. works, try 2.

This is especially true if you have a series of product offerings. Use 1 P.S. to call attention to the ease of ordering, the other to a special offer good for only a limited time. Repeating phone numbers, expiration dates, and other key factors is always good in the P.S.

Some Thoughts About Graphics

70. Whenever possible, photographs should be used over illustrations because photos are more believable, realistic, detailed, informative.

There are instances where a drawing or illustration is better, usually because of a copy point you wish to make. Generally, if you have good photography, use it.

71. A mix of photography with illustrations will work well.

A photo series may show people in action using your product, with illustrations outlining the technical characteristics of the "black box" (which may be very important to an engineer, architect, or technical person). Here photographs and illustrations work together effectively.

72. Photos should add to your message. Art for art's sake is NOT necessary.

Many lead generation packages are void of all art or graphics. Copy only. If a picture is worth 1,000 words, show me a picture of the

Constitution! A picture does NOT carry your message in direct response without strong copy.

Make sure there is a reason for the graphics—a sales reason.

73. *Use illustrations or line art to show quality details, product benefits, and suggested applications of your product, especially where good photography is impossible or impractical to obtain.*

Line art works very well in the presentation of technical products, certain food products where print reproduction quality is questionable (such as newspapers), architecture, fashion, and any easy-to-understand product. And for services where there is no tangible product to picture.

74. *A good picture works to support good copy.*

Pictures with people should be used in your catalogs, brochures, and print ads to add interest, invite inspection, dramatize problems. Packages with people pictures are always more interesting than those without. Many of your select audience will be open to helping attractive-looking people. Use good photography.

75. *In every case where photographs or line drawings are used, a caption under or beside the illustration is a necessity.*

It is not an option. Do not leave the picture or drawing "hanging" so readers have to guess what is happening or why they should look at it at all. Without a caption, you have a 50-50 chance your prospect will miss the benefit you are showing.

76. *Use easy-to-read type—a clean, clear, crisp typeface.*

Serif typefaces are much easier to read for anything you hold in your hand, like this book, a magazine, a newspaper, a piece of mail, or a brochure. Serifs are the "feet" or hooks on letters.

Sans serif type is best for things you read far away, such as a sign, a poster, or a billboard. Sans serif is acceptable for headlines and boldface subheads in print and mail.

77. Use a sufficient size type as well. Absolute minimum size for a letter is 9 point.

Most of your readers wear glasses or contacts. There is a reason—they can't see! Make certain the type size is large enough to read easily. The type size in this book is 11 point.

78. Just as paragraphs should not be too long (to make for easier reading) blocks of body copy should not be too wide.

One measure is to keep each line of copy to between 40 and 60 characters. Blocks that are too narrow are also difficult to read; anything less than 20 characters should be avoided.

79. Break up large blocks of copy with bold subheads, columns, photographs, illustrations, or some other design.

Graphics can play a very large part in making your message easy to read and understand.

80. Avoid reverse type—white on a dark background.

Why? Because it is hard to read, even with large serif type. Small amounts of reverse type, say up to 25 words or so, are fine. It is when you get long blocks that readers turn off.

81. Your coupon in a space ad and a response card in direct mail should be square or rectangular.

Please, no coupons shaped as triangles, circles, people, or "things." They are hard to read and, even more important, harder to use!

In space ads, ask for right-page placement in magazines and in newspapers, preferably on the lower right part of the page. Position the coupon on the lower outside edge, usually the lower right.

Should you experiment with other coupon locations? Sure! Try the top of the page, the center, and the top outside corner. Tradition and testing have found the bottom is best—which does not lock out new ideas. However, I do recommend that you do not "float" your coupon in the middle of the page—results are usually disastrous.

82. *Your order form in your mail-order package or catalog must be clear, easy to find, and easy to read.*

It should have sufficient space to list all the information you require to fulfill the order. Give clear, simple, easy to understand instructions. Put *both* on the order form and adjacent to it.

83. *On your order form or response card, list your toll-free number or other telephone number, your fax, and your e-mail address.*

Allow your audience to respond to your offer in different ways, if they wish. Include your company name, logo, and complete mailing address, too, even if this information is elsewhere in the mail package or print ad. If the only element your prospects have is the reply device, make certain they have every opportunity to reply.

84. *Upper and lower case is easier to read than all UPPER CASE.*

Your headlines, subtitles, and other attention-getting areas in your brochure can use upper and lower case effectively—sometimes (in very short bursts) all UPPER CASE. Body copy should always be upper and lower.

Why? Well, ONCE YOU GET BEYOND A FEW WORDS OF A PASSAGE SET ENTIRELY IN CAPS IT CAN BECOME QUITE A CHORE TO READ. ESPECIALLY WHEN THE TYPE IS SET IN NARROW COLUMNS, AS IT OFTEN IS. *IT IS EVEN WORSE WHEN IT IS SET IN CAPITAL ITALICS!*

85. *Make different sections of your brochure look different. Make the two sides of each piece look different.*

Yes, they must "flow." They must look like they go together. By using screens and different rectangular blocks, borders, and other graphic devices to make the piece more interesting to read, you will gain more action.

The eye goes to anything out of the ordinary. The eye goes from dark to light, from large to small, from bright to drab. Try it.

86. This little trick always works: Handwritten notes get noticed.
A handwritten note in the margin or as the second P.S., to draw
attention to a specific point, will often increase your response. Try it.

87. Avoid the "crick in the neck" syndrome.
*A small amount of italic type can be pretty, and certainly italic typefaces
have their uses. Yet, long passages of type set in italics are a problem. It's not
that any one word is difficult to read, but the collective effect gets pretty tir-
ing. It's the "crick in the neck" syndrome.*

*88. The copy in your direct mail letter, your brochure, and your
print ad should be set ragged right, not with justified right
margins.*
With word processors and other mechanical capabilities, it is easy to
justify the right-hand margin. So, why not do it? Because it makes it
harder to read your message. Spacing between words is often
uneven. Your paragraph "jumps" around. Use ragged right margins;
they are easier to read.

*89. The Magazine Publishers Association, using data from a
Starch Tested Copy report, shows us how much effect position,
color, and size really have on response. And yes, the numbers
vary some year to year, magazine to magazine. Still . . .*
Table 7.1 offers words (and numbers) for thought. The base number is
100. Those positions with higher numbers enjoyed a greater readership. Those with a lower number had less readership. Of course, these
are averages. Your product in a specialty magazine will be different.

90. Type should be seen and not heard.
(Ideas for these 10 points stolen from a book by friends Ken Erdman
and Murray Raphel.)

- Type makes a first impression. Be sure yours is a good one.
- Type has personality—short, tall, skinny, fat, tough, weak,
plain, fancy. Which looks like your business?

Table 7.1 ■ Effect of Physical Factors on Response

Covers Versus Inside Page			
Inside position	100		
Second cover	118		
Third cover	118		
Fourth (back) cover	132		

Size of Ad			
Full page	100		
Half page	69		
2-page spread	128		

Color of Ad			
Black & white	100		
2-color	83		
4-color	141		

Size and Color Combined	Full Page	Half Page	Spread
Black & white	100	74	116
2-color	90	61	N/A
4-color	132	100	171

Left Versus Right Pages	Left Page	Right Page	
1 page, color	100	101	
1 page, black & white	100	100	

Bleed Versus Non-Bleed Ads	Bleed	Non-bleed	
1 page, color	115	100	
1 page, black & white	111	100	

Position in Magazine	Noted	Associated	Read Most
First third	105	103	93
Middle third	100	100	100
Last third	101	104	101

- Type has "sound." Lots of it, big and bold, is a SHOUT. Lesser and smaller is quiet. Some is uptown, some downtown. What sound do you want to make?
- Type creates mood. The Salvation Army needs to look poor if they expect donations. The Rolls dealership needs to look like what it is—rich. What are you?
- Type must be readable. Why any is not is a total mystery to me. Why have it if it can't be read? Don't pick any style or size that is unreadable.
- Type is background. Its purpose is to get you to read and understand the message, not to be the message. There is a big difference. Pick type to create atmosphere, not be atmosphere.
- Type should rarely be reverse. That means don't do white on black. It is too hard to read. Small amounts sometimes may be OK. But rarely.
- Type is family. Keep the family together. Don't mix typefaces on the same piece. You may get away with 2 complementary faces, but no more. And you may use different typefaces on different pieces inside the same package.
- Type breathes. White space between words and paragraphs is needed. Allow them to breathe, so they can be read easily.
- Type stands alone. Overprinting anything may be nice for art directors, but it is death to readers. Type is communication; let yours communicate.

91. *Rare indeed is the copywriter who is equally effective in direct marketing graphics and design.*

However, every copywriter should make a rough layout as a means of communicating with the art director. The copywriter's rough should be just that—rough, very rough. Some copywriters prefer to write headlines on the rough. Others simply give an indication to the art director of what the most important headlines and elements are and then suggest photography. By reviewing the elements identified in the copywriter's rough, the art director will immediately understand which selling points the copywriter feels should receive the greatest emphasis.

92. *"I can't save this copy!" says the art director.*

In direct response, graphics is a support tool. Superior art, photography, and illustrations cannot save poor copy, although it can make it much, much better.

Get your art director working with you early in your project. Let him or her know what you are planning, thinking. Get his or her ideas in the beginning; it will pay dividends when it comes time to create the final layout and design.

Creative by the Numbers: Wrap-Up

93. *The book of Genesis told the story of the creation of the world in 442 words.*

The Lord's Prayer is 68 words. Abraham Lincoln used 267 words for the Gettysburg Address. (By the way, an even 200 of the 267 words are 5 letters or fewer!)

The U.S. government produced a report on cabbage that totaled 29,911 words.

Enough said. Some powerful statements are brief. Some perfectly awful writing is far too long. Copy is not short or long—it is interesting or uninteresting. Period. Can 29,911 words on cabbage be interesting to anybody?

94. *Here are some ways to add some FLASH to your direct mail:*

- Use commemorative stamps.
- Use exciting color—such as a fire-engine red envelope.
- Use a color, glassine window cover to "hide" a secret message.
- Affix an "official" seal to the envelope.
- Use graphics on both sides of your outgoing envelope.
- Tape a folded note to the outside of your envelope.
- Use an entirely different format; make your mail look like a newspaper.

- Use a mix of photographs and drawings on your envelope and in your brochure. Even as part of an "illustrated" letter.

95. *Tossing pebbles 1 by 1 into a pond creates a ripple effect, which is much different than if you dumped a 1-ton boulder all at once!*

Add some drama and SPLASH to your promotion. Here are more ideas:

- Combine all the printing techniques you can dream of in 1 mail package—personalization, rub-offs, scratch 'n' sniff, embossing, a stamp sheet, and more.
- Mail in a paper sack, burlap bag, tube, box, or puffy envelope.
- Rather than the more conventional style, use a double-flap, bangtail, outgoing mailing envelope.
- Use an envelope that "falls apart," with die-cuts, perforations, and printing on the inside of the envelope.
- Run a short-time sweeps or other contest that closes in just 6 weeks.

96. *Time moves quickly in the eyes of your prospect.*

You have only 2–3 seconds to get attention with your direct mail; about 4 seconds with your ad in a newspaper; the same length of time with your e-mail message and on your Web site; and 13–17 seconds with a telemarketing call. If you do not grab your audience fast, they will pass you equally fast and go on to something else.

All of which means you had better be good! Your message—the teaser copy on your mail, the headline in your ad, your e-mail, your Web site, the opening of your telephone call—must do the job in a big hurry.

97. *Here is a checklist for writing and designing coupons, response forms, reply cards and envelopes, and order forms.*

Or, how to lead your customers to give YOU their business:

- □ Tell them exactly what you want them to do.
- □ Make it easy for them to respond.
- □ Make them an offer they can't refuse.
- □ Use bold graphics; show the product; show the offer.
- □ Use clear, crisp, concise, and positive copy.
- □ Get them involved; use action devices.
- □ Give them room to write!
- □ Include your company name, logo, address, phone and fax numbers, e-mail address, Web site, and URL on the coupon, the reply card, and the order form.
- □ Give them a guarantee.
- □ Have a limited time offer.
- □ Include 2 (or more) response forms, order cards, or coupons.
- □ Always AFTO (Ask for the Order)!

98. Power direct marketing is a people business. People make things happen. Although this is a time when both quality and service are "expected," we must always remember it is people who create quality and provide service.

Here is a list of 28 things to know about people:

- ■ People procrastinate over making any "thinking" decision. If it is going to take brain power, you are going to have to write stronger and say it better if you are to gain immediate action. You must give your audience a reason (or several) to respond now.
- ■ People are skeptical of anything new—new people, new products, new services, a new offer, your new idea or way to do something. Know that many times people are happy with just where they are today. If you want them to make a decision in your favor, present your message with a highly believable offer.
- ■ People follow leaders, companies and products that are leading or those who are "considered" leaders. Please note, if you can position yourself, your company, your product, or your offer as a leader, you will be way ahead of the game and your competition.
- ■ People prefer the comfort of unity: "two-getherness." Meaning people like to be with other people like them. That's why they

form groups with others of similar interests and backgrounds. It happens all around the world. Schools are built where there are families with kids. Restaurants are located where people need or want to be fed. Churches go up where people of that faith live. Know this about audiences: They group "two-gether."

■ People are sometimes flat-out lazy! Yes, all of us are lazy some of the time. Yet, there appears to be a breed of folk who practice laziness as a habit. Know that when you reach out to your marketplace and make it easy for people to do business with you, you can catch this lazy bunch.

■ People glance at, more than thoroughly read, what you present to them. Even when they ask you to send them something, much of the time your message is not read—it is looked at instead. Know this fact, then make your writing as easy to read as your audience wishes.

■ People say, "I don't understand this message." Well, of course they don't understand it; they didn't read it! What this says is you must go to extremes to make your message readable, so when it is read, it will be totally understandable.

■ People say, "I didn't ask you to send me this message." Possibly this is true. What is equally true is if you don't get your message to your audience, they will then complain they didn't hear from you. Do make certain your message goes to the right people every time, and you are much less likely to hear any complaints.

■ People say, "I've had a rotten day and feel really crummy." Everybody has a bad day now and then, which of course has nothing to do with anything. It is an excuse, not a reason, for not replying to your offer. But people will still say it. So, what do you do? Make your message a happy one!

■ People like grooves and formulas and niches. Lists of things are important and work well in power direct marketing: The 5 easy steps, a 4-point plan, 10 things to know. Give people a list—directions to follow—and there is a good chance you've got 'em.

■ People like the feeling of power and control. They want to make their own decisions. They want to feel that they are important. And, of course, they are! People are your prospects and your customers. Know that people are important.

▪ People respond best to limited time offers (which is most interesting, as LTOs take all power and control away). Offers with limits most often gain more response than those without. Limited time offers urge people to take action now, before the opportunity slips by.

▪ People worry over decisions and changes. They do "what if" thinking: "What if I make this change and it's wrong?" or "What if I make a decision in that direction and it doesn't work?" People worry. Take the worry away with a case history or two. Allow people to become comfortable with you.

▪ People avoid risks and threats. There are only a very few leading-edge people out there. Not many will make a move to something new before it is proven. Be aware of that and be persistent with your message. People also don't like to be threatened. You can convince, you can prove, you can persuade, you can even sell. Do not threaten.

▪ People give incomplete attention to your message—a message that would help them in decision making and risk avoidance. Simply, this means people don't listen either. We know they are not reading what you are writing, and they are not listening to what you are saying. No wonder they don't get it! Be aware of this and be prepared—in fact, plan—to repeat your message over and over, again and again, until they get it.

▪ People ask lots of questions. First, they ask questions about your offer. We know an offer is over and above features and benefits, and your audience wants to know all about it. Be prepared with answers. Think ahead to what questions are most important and provide the answers.

▪ People ask questions about benefits under the WAM (What About Me?) theory. What am I going to gain from buying this product or service from you? What are the benefits to me, my family or friends, my staff at the office, my company? This is not a selfish act, it is an honest response to your presentation. So, what do you do? Talk about what they will earn, save, make, enjoy, learn. Talk benefits.

▪ People ask questions about a guarantee of satisfaction. There are 2 parts to every guarantee: First is, that the product will work, do what it is supposed to do, or the service will be supplied. That much of the guarantee is assumed.

The second part of the guarantee is the personal part: "What if I buy, and you provide, but I'm still not happy? What will you do to make me happy?" A guarantee of satisfaction is mandatory in power direct marketing. Period!

■ People ask questions about facts and figures that prove your statements. They want to believe you, they really do. Show your marketplace you have proof at your fingertips. Hide nothing. Prove your presentation with facts and figures.

■ People generalize from what they consider "acceptable fragments." They draw conclusions based on incomplete information, partly because they have not read or listened to your message. Partly because they want to believe you, no matter what you say. You must realize that many times people make a decision they regret later, and it will be YOUR responsibility.

■ People are suspicious of perfection. If something is "perfect," they look immediately for the imperfection. Research has taught us that people are most comfortable with an 85% level of knowledge; this is where things are most believable. This does not mean people don't want the best. It does mean you don't have to be perfect to be successful.

■ People prefer a little less information, not so much knowledge. Why? Because there is so much to know, many people have decided to be selective. And because they want to make their own decisions. They want to seek out what is important to them and then ask for the details. So they can come to their own conclusions; so they can feel that they are in charge of the situation. You must be prepared for a dialogue with your customers and prospects at the level they wish to communicate.

■ People do want to trust you, they really do. People want to believe. Which puts the burden of proof and believability on you. Testimonials and references, other people saying good things about you, will help you build trust. You must perform up to standards. Sometimes you set them; your customer always does. You must know what your audience expects.

■ People want the heart and warmth and emotion and feel-good of the sales process. They want the touch. Reach out and touch your marketplace. Let them know you care. Be personal. Communicate. And do it often. Hold their hand. Be their teddy bear, their security blanket. Touch your customers.

■ People's responses to any message are in direct proportion to their personal identification with you, your product or service, your company. If you are known in your marketplace, you will gain more new business and keep more current business than if you are not. Be active. Be seen. Let your audience know who you are.

■ People ask questions about the next step. "Okay, I agree. What happens next? What do you do? What do I need to do?" People want to know the process. You must make certain they do.

■ People ask questions about timing. They want to know how long this process is going to take. They say, "If I make this decision today, how long will it be before something happens?" Tell your audience all about the timing.

■ People always want to be sought after, talked with, they want you to AFTO (Ask for the Order). No, most people do not like to be sold, but they sure do like to buy. You must make 100% certain with power direct marketing that they know you want them to buy from you. Always AFTO.

These are 28 important things to know about people as you prepare creative for successful power direct marketing.

99. *The last thing you do creatively is check to see whether the components of your mailing package reinforce each other.*

Do the letter, brochure, lift letter, and order form complement each other? Do they work together? In your space advertisement, do the headlines and graphics work together? Are the benefits easily grasped and understood? Are the coupon and/or tip-in business reply card and toll-free number prominent?

With your catalog, can the customer find all the vital information necessary to place an order? Do the graphics support the sales-oriented copy? Does your Web site encompass all of these factors, as it must for you to gain maximum results?

Does your message come across clearly to your audience, to give you the best opportunity to get the maximum results? Does it get your prospect involved sufficiently to take action, and to do so now? Did you ASK FOR THE ORDER?

Remember, it's not creative unless it sells. Which means the creative process, both the copy and the art, must "walk" your customer or prospect through the process toward a sale. Toward measurable results and power direct marketing.

Chapter 8

PRODUCTION/MEDIA

IF EVERYTHING SEEMS TO BE GOING WELL, YOU'VE OBVIOUSLY OVERLOOKED SOMETHING

■ ■ ■

Power direct marketing includes the techniques you select to produce your direct response marketing program: direct mail; fulfillment packages; sales support materials; point of purchase; premiums and specialties; inserts; 1-, 2-, or 4-color, the quality of print and broadcast production. All of these can dramatically influence your success in 2 important ways:

- Your level of awareness, image, and readership will be significantly affected by the quality you choose.
- The way you actually produce the package will have a major effect on the cost of your direct marketing program.

Production is the seventh point of The 8ight Point Market Action Plan.

■ Some Questions to Consider ■

Here are questions to think about as you plan your direct response production and select the correct media:

1. Which media are best suited for communicating your product benefits? For motivating prospects to action?
2. Which media will best reach your target audience?
3. Can these media be used effectively for direct response marketing?
4. Is the product to be marketed geographically? If so, what are the boundaries of the media you're using?
5. Can the media selected be used regionally? Nationally? Internationally?
6. Are there seasonal variations in expected response levels that will affect scheduling?
7. Will scheduling be affected by other activities within your company, such as your sales promotion and advertising plans?
8. How much space is needed to present your offer? How much time is needed to sell the offer, present the product, and maximize response?
9. What media mix will produce the desired sales volume results within your budget parameters and time frame— *and* meet your marketing criteria?
10. What is the relative cost efficiency and response potential of each medium?
11. Within a particular medium, which vehicles will reach your target audience most effectively and efficiently?
12. What response must be generated to achieve the target cost per inquiry and cost per close?
13. In space advertising, is the editorial environment compatible with your product? Is other advertising/ marketing in the same vehicle compatible with your

company? Where is the competition? As applicable, ask
the same questions for direct mail lists, trade shows, and
other tools.

14. By adding additional media, what is the duplication of
audience? The frequency? Is frequency beneficial?
Necessary?

15. Where does your current customer base fit in your overall marketing program for the next 12 months?

After you have given yourself comfortable answers to each applicable question, please don't rock back on your heels, pass the baton
to the production coordinator, and go fishing. It just doesn't work
that way. As Sandy McCormick, founder of McCormick Oil & Gas,
said: "Organize yourself so that when everything that can possibly
go wrong goes wrong twice, you are still in business."

Production of anything printed seems to offer endless possibilities for things to go wrong. This is especially true for direct mail
because you have so many variables, so many different elements
coming together, there are countless ways for things to go wrong.
And they do!

Just think about it. First you have copy, the message itself, with
all of the many different ways for it to be produced and presented.
Then there is the art, the graphics that make the copy better. This
includes layout and design, photographs and illustrations.

Next are the physical factors, including all the various paper
stocks, colors, sizes, and weights; envelopes in many varieties; literally hundreds of color combinations; 1-, 2-, and 4-color printing.
With overlays, screens, and more.

Throw in a test or 2—let's say a twin offer and 4-list test as outlined in Chapter 6. Which means coding and carefully enclosing the
right pieces together so the test is valid.

Is it any wonder those in charge of pulling all of this together
sometimes pull their hair out? These folks must wear many hats. As
Murphy says, "Anything that can go wrong will go wrong."

■ CREATIVE AND PRODUCTION CHECKLIST ■

Planning the creative approach and the media mix—the message carriers—happens simultaneously. They come together as one. Getting the work physically accomplished comes afterward. It is important to begin coordination early. A "working with" attitude must prevail between the account and creative team that are developing the program and the production team that has the responsibility to make it all happen.

The good folks of Mayne Associates of Lafayette, California; the catalog production group at Inmac, a mail-order computer supply house; and Polly Pattison, a publication design consultant, have each supplied me with a few ideas that will help you and your creative and production teams work better together. Special assistance has come from Erin Prell, a professional production coordinator and good friend. Erin, because she is personally familiar with many of the projects I have been involved with, brought me up to date on production.

So, I've combined my own hands-on experience (including some wonderfully successful as well as outrageously horrible programs) with knowledge from the professionals to come up with 2 dozen IDEAS.

Plan in Advance

Plan everything, every detail. Think about all the variables and options. Write them down, look at the list, and add to it. There is no such thing as too much knowledge.

If the deadlines are tight, it is even more important to plan ahead so you can decide where sacrifices will need to be made.

If the campaign is complex, you need a list to make 110% certain you have included everything in its place. Just as an architect needs a blueprint to build a house, you need a checklist to ensure you've covered every production base. Plan in advance.

Bring in Your Suppliers Early

Talk to your most experienced heads. Ask for their input. Get their technical expertise early on in your development stage. Do this before you get committed to a single concept that may not be the best way for you to go—before it becomes too late or too expensive to make the needed changes.

Set Schedules

Having a schedule is not an option; *it is mandatory* for everyone. An entire section of The 8ight Point Plan is devoted to scheduling—that's how important it is to the success of your direct response program.

Many times we do have a schedule. We're serious about it, and then something falls out of line, something "breaks" along the way. Do we adjust? Sometimes. Many times we just pressure the production team to "meet the deadline" and then wonder why quality is not up to standard.

Here is a rule of thumb schedule for various direct mail activities. Build these times into your schedule:

Activity	Weeks
List selection/rental	2–5
Rough copy	1–3
Rough layouts	1–2
Approval	1–2
Finished graphics	1–3
Order/receive paper	2–8
Order/receive envelopes	1–5
Print letters/simple pieces	1–3
Personalized package letters	2–4
4-color printed materials	2–4
2-color printed materials	1–3
Lettershop	1–2

Of course, all of this depends on many things. One of the big items is quantity: the larger your mailing, the more time you need to schedule; the more personal the package, the more time it will take.

Another factor is people. Don't rush people. People make mistakes and mistakes cost. Stick to your plan. Enforce your realistic deadlines and then, be tough.

Work from Your Budget

Good professionals are problem solvers. It's their job to know how to get things done. They know (so do you) that good ideas cost money. There is no such thing as a free lunch.

Even though one expert may make a marvelous recommendation, you have to live within your budget. Don't throw away a good idea; save it for next time or the time after that. Consider every idea—many will save you money.

Little things, such as a slight change in paper size, can be worth a lot to you. Consider everything and then decide the best road for you and this program.

Shop for Services

Shop just as you would for anything. Give complete instructions at the beginning. Start by writing specs for every job and then ask questions. Get quotes. Make certain you understand what you are asking and what you are buying. Consider dividing the tasks among several direct response printers and lettershops. Don't assume all printers are alike—they are not.

Using specialists from a number of sources may save you money, as long as you keep control and can maintain your schedule.

Copy Fit as You Write

This is directed to copywriters. By working with production from the beginning, it is much easier to make certain your copy will fit where it is supposed to fit. Know how many characters fill one line (40 to 60, please—it is much easier to read). Know your limits, and copy fit as you write.

Make a Dummy

A dummy is a "sample" of your package with all of the elements cut and folded to final size and with the weight of paper you will be using. Make it as close to the final and real package as possible. Why? For at least 2 reasons:

- It helps both the copywriter and the art director see how the package and all its pieces come together—how they fit. It is important they do! For example, a dummy helps you be certain the response card fits the response envelope.
- You need to check legal and postal requirements. Today, almost anything is legal when it comes to weight, size, and other factors. Yet, there are great savings by going with automation.

This is most certainly true for mail in post offices around the world and is an obvious necessity for anything else you print—brochures, literature, catalogs, sales pieces. Ditto for advertising in magazines and newspapers; you must know the specs.

A dummy will help you do it right. You don't want any surprises.

Be Acutely Aware of Machine Requirements

Today, we can truly get anything we want done somewhere, some way, somehow. At a cost of money or time.

To understand machine requirements, it is best to pass your dummy package by the experts first—the lettershop if it is direct mail. They will help you gain the maximum result for your effort.

If you can get some machine to do it, it sure saves on wear and tear of mind and body—not to mention the budget.

Use Standard Everything Where Practical

Sure, it is exciting to use an odd shape or size envelope or package. The only problem is it may not fit in the mail box, may not work with the machinery, or may require hand work.

This is not to say the different or unusual doesn't have a place in direct marketing—it does. Just make sure it is worth the extra effort and cost.

Use Copy That Can Stand Alone

Copy is king in direct response. The graphics can (and should) make the copy better, just as with television and radio. Even with the same message, TV is more exciting because of graphics.

Yet, unless the copy is good, the art director cannot be expected to save it. If it is bad to begin with, it will still be bad afterward. What do graphics do? The prime purpose of graphics in direct marketing is to get the copy read.

Illustrate First with Photographs

Use people in pictures and captions underneath. Why? Because research indicates photographs are more believable. They enjoy higher readership when compared to illustrations. And, why captions? Because they too get read. Your audience learns quickly what it is you are telling them, sharing with them. They get your message.

Does this mean that art doesn't have a place in direct response? Absolutely not! It most certainly does. Sometimes a mix of line art and photographs makes for a better mail package, brochure, flyer, fulfillment piece, or technical brochure.

Consider Stock Art and Photographs

There are times when using what is available from a stock house is just as good, if not better, than going to the time and effort of creating your own originals. Keep ego out of it; it may save you a considerable bundle.

Consider Borders, Backgrounds, Corners, and Other Decorations for "Dress"

Any decent-size print production house has scores, if not hundreds, of type ornaments. And, of course, thousands of options are available on disk.

Your mail, brochures, and print ads may all benefit from some "dressing." Know what is available—and use them where they fit. They too can offer a cost savings over original art.

Use Other Possible Cost-Saving Graphic Ideas

Consider using colored paper stock as a substitute for extra press runs or a second color. Color stock costs more than white, yet sometimes the net result will be a savings if you eliminate a press run. And sometimes not! Depending on what you're producing, it may be less expensive to print a color than to buy the paper.

Consider "simulated" die-cuts instead of the real thing. Little things, such as rounding corners and drilling holes, scoring on the press and perforations, all give you an action look, without the heavy expense. Try it.

Avoid special inks. Unless you have a truly unusual color combination and/or your board of directors is particularly fussy, stay with the standard PMS colors. Out of the many hundreds available, you can certainly find what you want and save the extra cost and press time.

If nothing else, use screens of your basic ink color. Screens can take the place of the second color. Overlapping screens of 2 colors can even replace a third or fourth color.

"Gang" Your Production Stages

Gang separate your photos. Gang run printing jobs. Choose your photographs with uniform contrasts and then do standard reductions.

When you print more than one piece at the same time, on the same press, costs drop dramatically. All of this applies when it is practical. At least think about it up front—it saves a little time and a lot of money.

There have been a couple "avoids" in our list; here come some more. "Avoids" are things that can get you into trouble. This does not mean you should never do these things; it does mean look at the situation carefully. Then decide whether it works for you.

Avoid White Space

Avoid blank pages, accordion folds, and avoid "fancy." Avoid things that add nothing to the success of your direct mail or brochure. It's not that some of these ideas aren't worthwhile on occasion—they are. In each case, you have to decide if they really help your sales message to be understood.

On blank pages, remember: nobody reads the white space. Allow your copy to breathe, yes. But white space for the sake of artistic beauty wins no awards in direct response. The graphics are to support the copy, make it better, more readable—not replace it.

Avoid Tight Registrations, Overprinting Photos, and Bleeds and Heavy Ink

Tight registrations require rules around photos, which means extra care in the printing process. It costs money.

Why, oh why, anyone overprints photos with type I'll never understand. It destroys the photo and you can't read the copy!

Bleeds and heavy ink are similar to tight registrations; if the feel of the piece requires it, fine. It just takes more time and costs more money. Be sure you can justify both. Remember, awards hang on walls. The money goes to the bank.

Avoid Reverse Type, Italics, ALL CAPS

A little reverse works well, but too much is unreadable. Italic in small amounts adds emphasis to your message; too much is unreadable.

Uppercase letters are fine in small doses, but too much is unreadable. You want your message read, so give it to your audience in the most readable format possible.

Square, Clean, Accurate, and Neat (SCAN)

It's amazing how sloppy we can get in this business. It's also amazing how our sophisticated production processes pick up exactly what we give them. As in the computer industry, GIGO (garbage in, garbage out). The same thing happens in direct response production. Our computer technology allows us to do things never dreamed of earlier in the 20th century. This same technology allows us to make more mistakes.

So, yes, it does take a little longer to apply the SCAN formula. Do it.

Use Serif Typefaces for Handheld Materials

This is about physiology—our bodies—not marketing, direct marketing, or advertising. Studies done in Germany, Canada, Australia, and the United States have taught us some things about our eyes and reading: serif type is better for anything you expect or want to be read. Use it where you have lots of copy. (And copy is the rule rather than the exception in direct response.)

Does sans serif type have a place in direct marketing? Probably yes, but not if I can help it! Why do anything that makes it more difficult for your audience to get your message? Sans serif is used heavily in certain media, such as outdoor posters, bus cards, signs, and many audiovisual aids such as slides and overheads.

For readability, use the serif typefaces. Out of all that are available you'll find several you like.

Note: For copy on computer screens, meaning e-mail and Web sites, it's a toss-up which type is better because the screen is somewhere in distance between handheld and other materials. It's farther away than a book, but it's closer than a poster. For me, your Web pages and e-mail should use the same "rules" that apply to direct mail.

Here are some thoughts on type size. Make sure your type is large enough to be read easily. Most newspapers use 8-point type. My suggestion is to use 9-point or larger; I personally prefer 10- or even 12-point type. Anything smaller than 8 point is too difficult to read. Which may be just fine if you're forced to include the legal requirements or other necessary information nobody reads anyway. (There are laws about all of this; make sure you know and follow them.)

Look at your audience and decide whether a few more pages of larger type might be worth it. There is a reason most of the world wears glasses!

Avoid Dating Materials

Unless it is absolutely necessary, don't put a specific date on anything printed. It immediately becomes dated, which may mean a perfectly good piece of literature or a direct mail package becomes old before its time.

A little trick I learned is to include the DAY of the week on the letter in the package. The day—let's say Tuesday—gives a feeling of currency. It can't be more than a week old, yet that same piece can be used as is for months.

Include Full Information

Put your corporate name, logo, complete address, area code/telephone and fax numbers, e-mail address, Web site URL, and any special project coding on every piece in your direct mail and fulfillment packages. Also, include this same data in every print ad you put in newspapers and magazines and on your brochures, flyers, take-ones, and handouts. On everything.

Why? So that if any one of your pieces is separated from the others your audience can still find you. Be easy to do business with; be available.

Make Any Changes Early

Don't design on press. Some people truly cannot visualize a package until they see it, which is another reason a dummy package or tight layout can be so important. But, even with a dummy, some people at the approval level decide at the last minute that something just has to be changed.

My rule is this: If it is truly an error (wrong, a mistake), then it gets corrected. If it is a desire, a want, a feeling, you get to pay for it. It will cost in money and probably in time. You may miss your place in line or you may miss an important "drop-dead" date. Your choice.

Put It All in Writing

This way, everyone knows what to expect and when. Because production people are busy, many times with a number of balls in the air, they tend to prefer not to put everything in writing. Don't do that to yourself or let it happen to you. By now you can certainly understand the advantage of having all the decisions, directions, and dates in writing. If for no other reason than to catch something that fell through the crack.

▪ IN SUMMARY ▪

I have not attempted to recommend, suggest, or debate pros and cons on the way to do anything or to discuss the very detailed technology that is available today.

For someone like me, who has difficulty closing the ironing board or hanging a picture straight, production itself is something of a miracle. Frankly, I don't really understand how it all happens, how it all comes together. And you know what? I don't care! I do care that it happens within a reasonable schedule for a fair cost. *How* is of no real interest.

This attitude says you, like me, must have on your team—either inside your organization or out—someone like Erin Prell, or David Ohringer, or . . . People who understand the options and are capable of making the best decision when it comes to an either/or choice. People who know how to buy and who understand paper, the envelope business, printing in all its various formats. Who know when you can do it "down and dirty" and when it must be five stars.

People who can negotiate with brokers. Who understand what real deadlines are as opposed to those we artificially throw up from time to time. Who can first understand a budget and then work within it.

People who have or will build a stable of connections, like those suppliers who will walk the extra mile when it is needed. Who you can rely on to do what they say, by when they say, for the agreed-on amount.

People who can talk with copywriters and art directors and will work with account service and marketing communications folks.

This is a big list, a strong job description. And because the assignment and responsibility is large, you need a "big" person to do it.

Let's end this section with an interesting note from my friend Erin Prell: "In spite of our new reliance on computers and a few changes at the post office, production hasn't changed that much in the many years I've been in the business."

So, power direct marketing includes production as one of the important elements of The 8ight Point Market Action Plan because production is a key step in making direct response programs work. And work well.

Answer the questions to consider, review the creative and production checklists, then make certain you have people on your team who can pull it all together with you.

Chapter 9

ANALYSIS/MEASUREMENT

WINNING ISN'T EVERYTHING, BUT WHO CARES ABOUT ALL THAT OTHER STUFF?

■ ■ ■

Did you know that Americans buy 750 tons of cauliflower, use 313 million gallons of fuel, spend $200,000 on roller skates, and eat 200 million pounds of fresh fruit every day?

These startling facts—along with many others (6,000 teenagers lose their virginity; 50,000 television sets are bought and 20,000 are thrown away; 1,250 tonsils are taken out, along with 850 appendixes)—come to us by way of a book called, appropriately, In One Day: The Things Americans Do in a Day, *by Tom Parker (Houghton Mifflin).*

On the average day, the book says Americans make 110 holes-in-one, smoke 85,000 pounds of marijuana, jog 28 million miles, make 100,000 speeches, and publish 125 new books.

Interesting as it is, we're not sure exactly what to do with this information. Dropping a few of these facts at a cocktail party might liven things up—or stop conversation cold. Statistics junkies will revel in the facts themselves, and there's something to be said for that.

They do demonstrate that there are a lot of Americans out there pursuing many different tastes and interests—but you probably knew that already.

Perhaps the most amazing fact is on the cover: "In one day Americans print enough counterfeit money to buy 30,000 copies of this book." At $7.95, that's $238,500. It sounds like more.

From an editorial in the
Los Angeles Times

▪ Busy, Busy, Busy ▪

People have been measuring things for the 1,000 lifetimes we've been on earth. Some sort of formal housing has been around for over 150 lifetimes. The measurement of time has been happening for 80-plus lifetimes.

"Modern" communication has been available to us for less than 3 lifetimes. And we have enjoyed the speed and comfort of worldwide transportation as we know it today for less than a single lifetime.

Things happen rapidly. Every day a new book is published someplace in this world every 4 minutes—about 360 per day. Worldwide, 24 people will be born in the 6 seconds it takes you to read this sentence.

In the United States, 1.3 million frozen dinners are eaten daily. The mighty retailer, Sears, talks to 2.2 million people every day. The U.S. Postal Service delivers over 640 million pieces of mail 6 days a week, 55 million of them catalogs.

Around the globe, 2 billion telephone calls are made every day, about half of them in North America. And while those calls are being made, 5 million paper clips are being twisted. All in just one day.

A balance between lifetime measurement and daily measurement is needed. Lifetime measurements are too long; daily measurements are too short. Measurability of results—analysis—is not only desirable and possible, it is an absolute necessity. How else can you know what is going on in your marketplace? The word is *accountability.*

Direct marketing allows you to enjoy the benefit of knowing what happens, of measuring and analyzing. You want the telephone to ring with orders and leads. You want business reply cards returned. You want coupons redeemed. You want the order forms completed and mailed. You want the donations to come in. You want some direct physical action that allows for accountability, from your Web site, the mail box, the telephone. This is what direct response is all about.

Obviously you analyze and measure what happens at the end of your program. Sure, you do to-date counting as you are moving through the program, and the final analysis happens when the program is over.

But the planning for analysis must be done early in the initial organizational stages. Then, when you get to the finish line, you have in place all the tools to measure, to account for what has happened. This allows you the opportunity to count, to measure, to analyze, and to plan again for the future. For the next program.

Analysis is the last point of The 8ight Point Market Action Plan.

■ MURPHY AND SOME OTHER "LAWS" ■

The First Law of Statistics: If the statistics don't support your viewpoint, you obviously need more statistics.

The Second Law of Statistics: Given enough statistics, you can prove anything.

Two of Murphy's Laws

Direct marketing by definition is response oriented. The time and effort and money invested in developing and executing programs can be measured. In the final analysis, direct response is judged on its ability to achieve specific goals effectively and efficiently.

Contrary to the laws of Murphy, you're not looking for statistics to prove anything in direct response. You're analyzing a program to find out what happened! There is a big difference.

Countless surveys, both inside and outside the marketing and advertising community, all too frequently show that top management is skeptical of the sales value of marketing. Maybe because these same management people are familiar with Murphy. Maybe because direct marketing is foreign to them. Maybe because they don't understand telemarketing. Because of these beliefs, they look at marketing generally and direct marketing specifically as "fat," rather than muscle and strength. They see it as something they can't live with—or without!

One way to change this is with results—real results, measurable results, results you can do something with. Results come not from information, not from opportunities, not from discussion and review. Results come from the planned activity of commitment. Commitment early in your direct marketing program that you will measure what happens in your program and then take appropriate steps. Direct response does not allow you the option of ignoring results. To be successful in direct marketing, you must include in your plan measuring what happens—analysis.

You need to analyze the results. The purpose is to decide the next best steps to take; where to go next with your marketing efforts; what direction to take; whether you should make improvements or corrections and, if so, how much; whether you should make wholesale changes, go 180 degrees in the other direction. You want to find out what happened.

The beauty of direct response is it allows you to *prove* what works and what does not. It has been noted by many marketers over the years: "I know only half my advertising is working. The problem is I don't know which half." Not so with direct marketing. You know what is working and what is not because you plan and measure.

Direct marketing is accountable. You are not required to wait and wonder what happened. You know quickly by the response to your offer. And by analyzing the response, you can determine what is happening—now!

You count the number of visits to your Web site and the number that turn into responses and orders. You count the calls to your toll-free number and the faxback forms received. You count the business response card leads you get through the mail, the orders for your new product, the donations to that special cause or capital project, the coupons redeemed at your store, the traffic at your trade show booth. You know what happened.

With these answers you are able to evaluate the level of success of your campaign against your objectives and the return on your investment.

▪ 2 QUESTIONS THAT DESERVE AN ANSWER ▪

Marketing measurement is the effectiveness of a specific piece of direct mail or a full campaign, a direct response ad in a single publication or with a full schedule, broadcast media, a trade show—any and all media measurement is what you're looking for. Two questions come immediately to mind when you begin to talk about analysis and measurement. Let's look at each separately.

What Can I Expect in the Way of Response?

Good question, and the answer is, "I don't know." Another answer—equally correct—is, "It depends."

Why these evasive answers to an honest question? Why can't I at least give you a formula? For the same reason a doctor doesn't tell you what's wrong with you by looking and listening alone. Your accountant doesn't tell you what your taxes will be before working on your books. A jury doesn't come in with a verdict until they've heard all the evidence in the case.

In every instance where direct marketing is the discipline used to achieve an objective, there are too many factors to give you a flat answer (or really any answer) until more is known.

What about averages? In fact, it is literally dangerous to analyze your program in terms of averages. Averages may be fine for some things, but not direct response analysis. Are you average? No, of course not. Averages are just numbers, nothing more, and they mean just about that much in direct marketing. They might serve as a rough guide only. They should not be used to justify a direction or focus for your campaign.

It is far better, especially when you have a new product or service, when you are breaking into a new market, or when your response values vary greatly from low to high, to calculate the *median* value of your new lead, or that first donation, or first order. The median is the value that has half (50%) of all responses above it and the other half below. Calculate the median and use that figure for your projections, further testing, and the campaign rollout.

How can you get a number to work with? In the early planning stages of your program, when you need to think about budgets, fulfillment, manpower, and other elements of a complete campaign, how can you make an educated guess as to what to expect in the way of response? Fortunately, there are guidelines. Here are a few ideas:

- Start by looking inside your own company. What direct response programs have you run in the last year that might give you a fresh idea for this program?
- What about your industry? Are there publications specifically about your industry group?
- Does your industry have a trade association, maybe a special research department?
- The public library exists to provide information. It may be a good place to look.
- Local colleges and universities often have a department in your field; see if they can help.
- The Direct Marketing Association, its various councils, and Information Central service have a wealth of data available.
- If you're not in direct competition, maybe your business neighbor can help. You'll never know until you ask.

- The wonderful World Wide Web has scores of sources for you to search. It will take no more time, and maybe less, than a visit to your local library. And it is very likely to have more data than you could imagine or use.
- Lastly, use your own gut feeling. This is your company and your product we're talking about. You haven't been developing this program in a vacuum. What do YOU think is going to happen? What can you logically and rationally expect to be the response to your offer, directed to the right audience at this time?

There is information available in the marketplace. You may have to dig a little to find exactly what you want; most likely you will find something to guide you.

How Many Times Must I Make My Offer?

How many pieces of direct mail should I send; how many times should I run this space or broadcast ad?

Let's approach this from the advertising, public relations, or sales promotion side of the desk. If a key trade show in your industry was scheduled as a 4-day event, would you only exhibit the first day? Of course not. Why? Simply because you couldn't reach all your prospects in 1 day.

How many prime-time television commercials do you know of that ran only 1 time? Can you name 3? (Many people can probably name 1 or 2—rarely can anyone give me a third.)

How many times is a space ad run only 1 time, in only 1 magazine or newspaper? What about outdoor posters—do you put up only 1 board in only 1 location? Use only 1 bus card?

You get the idea. That just isn't how you do it. One of anything rarely gets the job done. The same principle applies to direct marketing: that is, repetition will increase your reputation. The more often your message is seen or heard, the more likely you are to gain a positive response. It only makes common sense.

The prime difference between advertising and what we in direct marketing do is that we carefully target our message. It is NOT for everyone; it is only for a few. We select our audience and direct our message and offer to them alone, rather than the large mass of everyone. Which gives us a leg up on knowing what happens, in measuring and analyzing our results.

As with the first question, I don't know the answer to this question, either. And again, it really does depend. For American Medical International, a hospital financial management firm, an 8-part direct mail series to hospital administrators (1 piece of mail every 6 weeks) was very effective. In a previous life for my direct marketing agency, we did a 17-part direct mail series over 4 years. It worked and continued to work for 4 years.

Paul Bringe tells a story about a series of 6 letters sent to the same list, offering the same service each time. Factoring the results, here is what happened:

Mailing	Responses
#1	100
#2	73
#3	54
#4	43
#5	41
#6	29

The 6 mail packages brought a total of 340 replies. What would have happened had this series been a single mailing? It would have generated only 100 responses. By continuing, an additional 240 prospects replied.

Most programs that produce well the first time can be expected to continue to produce well. In the preceding example, the letters were mailed about 3 weeks apart, each with the same message using a new approach. The audience was the same, the offer was the same, the message was the same, yet stated a different way each time. The proof it works is in the measurable results.

If you're willing to settle for a 1-time reach of your offer to your audience, chances are you're missing a major part of the potential business available to you. You're leaving money on the table.

▪ Testing and Measuring— Some Questions to Consider ▪

Testing is the backbone of direct response marketing. Many times, you will hear that the 3 rules of direct response are: test, test, test.

Almost any question can be answered quickly, inexpensively, and finally by testing. This is the best way to get an answer—conduct a test. By testing you get a much better feel of what is really happening in the marketplace. Certainly better than personal prejudices or arguments around the conference table.

Testing is a means of getting information from the marketplace about the marketplace. Sometimes surveys, in-depth research, and focus groups can be helpful in direct response. I firmly believe you learn the most about what is happening in the marketplace by going to it and testing. By letting your audience tell you what they'll *really* do—not what they intend to do, or hope to do, or might do. What you want (and need) in direct response is direct, physical action.

And you can only get that by being there, not asking a few folks to answer several questions and then making a decision on direction and focus of your campaign. Only by being in the marketplace can you really know what to expect.

Measurement is an activity that has many options. You have a host of choices on what to offer, who to offer it to, when, and in what geographic region. You have a multitude of possibilities, sometimes too many. How do you decide what to measure, what's important to you, what's important to know? By asking questions and testing.

Testing will help you do the following:

- Design your total campaign and every project within it
- Choose between copy themes and graphic ideas
- Zero in on your most likely prospects
- Decide your greatest potential market
- Decide your best offer
- Determine what time of the year is best for your offer
- Decide if you should expand geographically
- Avoid unnecessary risks with your program
- Gather helpful information to improve your total program

Still, testing is not for everyone. Certainly not all the time. In business-to-business marketing, your potential audience often is too small to justify testing. Either you are in that particular marketplace or you are not. The rule of thumb here is you need a universe of about 20,000 names minimum to conduct an effective direct mail test, a test you can do anything with.

Sometimes timing prevents thorough testing. It is hard to test a special offer for Mother's Day. You either do it or you don't. And because the market changes so rapidly, what you did last year may not be "in" this year.

If a high portion of your total budget will be required to test an idea, an offer, even a list, maybe you shouldn't do the test.

Here are some questions to consider when you begin to think about testing and measurement:

- Who are our customers? What are their demographics?
- How does our customer buy, by what method?
- What does our customer consider value?
- What products or services best satisfy the needs of our best customers?
- Who is our best prospect to become our customer?
- Who are these prospects buying from now? Why?
- Does our current marketing program reach our preferred marketplace?

- Does our current marketing program reach the right individuals in that marketplace?
- Which creative offer and format produces the most positive quality action from our marketplace?
- What if response is higher or lower than expected, than needed?

If you are in mail order, you might also measure these factors:

- How long has this customer been a customer?
- When was the most recent purchase?
- What is the frequency of purchase?
- What is the average and median value of the purchases?
- What specific products were bought?
- How did we get this customer in the first place, by what means?
- How does he or she pay—credit cards, check/purchase order, or bill-me? On time?
- Is this customer active or inactive by our definition?
- What did it cost to get this customer?
- What is the lifetime value of this customer?

If high-quality lead generation is your objective, here are some test and measure elements to consider:

- How many responses were generated?
- What is the percentage of response rate?
- What is the response to each medium? How many by mail, how many by space ads, how many at the trade show?
- Which direct mail lists, magazine publications, or broadcast produced the highest quality response? Which produced the most response?
- How many leads were qualified?
- How many qualified leads converted to an order?
- What is the cost per conversion per each medium?
- What is the average order size? What is the median?

- What products or services were purchased?
- How many calls/contacts were needed before the first order?
- How many new customers were obtained? Compared to the total marketplace?
- Which market segments offer the highest potential? In business, which Standard Industrial Classification (SIC) codes?
- Why did this new customer become a customer?
- What will his or her buying frequency be?
- If the prospect did not become a customer, why not?
- What did it cost to get a new customer?
- What is the lifetime value of this customer?

No company needs to answer all these questions. Every marketing manager, director, or vice president needs to *consider* each question and the thought it brings.

▪ The Value of Lifetime Value ▪

Because "lifetime value" has been mentioned a couple of times, let's talk about it specifically and the meaning it brings to analysis. You must make every effort to determine the lifetime value of your customers. This knowledge is the lifeblood of any direct response program designed to generate leads and donations, build traffic, or sell via mail order. Even if you have to guess in the beginning, you need to take a stab at it.

In most direct marketing programs you are either talking with your current customers in an effort to gain more business from them, or seeking new business. In both instances, you are trying to establish an ongoing relationship, a continuing buy/sell situation. You are seeking more business from the same people you already do business with, and you are looking for additional and new business from others. Business that also will grow into a regular client relationship. In both cases, you're talking about lifetime value. How much this customer will be worth to you over a long period of time.

Some of the best companies at doing this—figuring and using lifetime value in their marketing programs—are department stores. They know how much you'll spend with them if they get 1 of their store credit cards into your hands.

Generally, credit card people—all of them—are equally good at doing this. American Express, Diners, VISA, MasterCard, and the oil companies know what to expect; they know your lifetime value.

Mail-order marketers and fund-raisers are 2 more groups who use lifetime value to good advantage. They know how much they *need* to invest and how much they *can* invest to get you as a customer or donor. They know over time you'll be a customer of value or a donor of importance.

As you plan your direct response campaign, consider lifetime value and the place it has in your program. As Michael LeBoeuf, professor of management at the University of New Orleans, says: "The big bucks aren't in making customers. They're in keeping customers."

▪ THE 4 KEYS TO SUCCESSFUL ANALYSIS ▪

It is now obvious that digging inside your program to measure its effectiveness is no easy task. Detailed analysis may be complex, sometimes even difficult. To make it easier, I've reduced the key parts to just 4 points:

1. Did the program work? And what was it that worked?
2. What did not work?
3. Why did what worked work, and why did what didn't work not work?
4. What are you going to do with all this KNOWLEDGE next time around?

Let's talk about these 4 points one by one.

Did the Program Work? What Worked?

Usually this is easy to determine. You have the response and can tell rather quickly whether the program was a success or not. You can tell what mailing lists worked, what publications gained the most positive response, which television advertisement generated the most orders, whether your Web site is doing the job, which package got the most donations, and which coupon had the highest redemption rates.

This part is fairly obvious because you set up your program to measure—to count the numbers of responses, the orders over the toll-free number, the sales with offer A versus offer B. You can tell what worked.

This is basic measurement. It allows you to analyze your total direct marketing effort. Learn from your direct response successes what worked.

What Did Not Work?

Sometimes this is easy; many times it is not. It is easy because in an A versus B situation, one clearly dominated over the other. There was a runaway winner—a direct mail package that garnered two-thirds or three-fourths of all the response, and it paid. A coupon in a print ad that not only gained a healthy response against total circulation of that particular publication, but generated leads that made staff happy because they were closing sales off this program.

In another instance, the same ad in another magazine or newspaper wasn't doing anything. It was a flop, a dismal failure. This example is black and white. It's easy to pick the winner and the loser.

What happens when you test 2 different packages or offers and your response looks like Table 9.1? Let's assume you're happy with 10 sales from 10,000 contacts. Which of these two packages or offers would you roll out for more and which one would you toss?

It depends. The cost per sale is lower for B because you had to make fewer contacts to get the 10 sales. Still, it could be you're pleased with the 5% sales ratio of A. Plus, for future contacts and sales you have 100 more leads to follow up.

Table 9.1 ▪ Comparative Analysis of Packages/Offers

	Audience Reached	Percent Reached	Number Response	Percent Sold	Number Sold
Creative Package or Offer Test A	10,000	2%	200	5%	10
Creative Package or Offer Test B	10,000	1%	100	10%	10

Tough decision, isn't it? Sometimes it is not black and white. Judgment, timing, the marketplace, the competition, your sales staff size and capabilities, fulfillment services, and many other factors all enter into the decision. In any case, no matter how you see this example, you need to determine what does *not* work for you.

Table 9.2 gives another example. This time, it's a 4-way mailing list test. Which list or lists wins in this example? How do you analyze the results from this list test?

With by far the most nixies, List #3 is still the clear winner. Why? Because with 15 sales to 10 for each of the other lists, it has to be the choice. What about the efficiency of List #4? With fewer leads, 10 sales were still made. And List #2? With more leads, only 10 sales were made. Yet these two lists had a very low and acceptable nixie rate. Further, if you're satisfied with 10 sales from each 5,000 mailing, then *all* the lists are good for your purpose—you achieved your objective. In this example, the undeliverable mail isn't a factor because you reach your goal of 10 sales per 5,000 contacts.

Table 9.2 ▪ Comparative Analysis of Mailing Lists

List	Number Mailed	Nixies*	Percent Nixies	Leads Generated	Sales Made
#1	5,000	635	12.70%	100	10
#2	5,000	210	4.20%	110	10
#3	5,000	825	16.50%	100	15
#4	5,000	145	2.90%	80	10

*Nixie is a direct marketing term for undeliverable mail, mail that cannot be delivered because of an incomplete address or similar problem.

Of course, it is easy to draw the correct conclusion that the more mail delivered, the better your opportunity to get good leads from a good list—and consequently more sales. In this case, however, the list with the most nixie mail worked best.

Why Did Some Things Work, and Others Not?

Good friend Freeman Gosden, Jr., has done an entire direct marketing book on "why," because it is important to continued success in direct response. You need to find out why things happen so you can repeat the good things and eliminate the others.

It is not difficult to find out the good part of why—why what worked did work. How do you do this? Simply ask your customers. In a mail, telephone, or in-person interview, you ask them why. Because they are your customers, they'll tell you.

Your customers are your best source of what is going on in your marketplace. If they've just bought from you, it is likely they've shopped around and know what's being offered. They may know more than you do about what is really happening out there (hopefully not, but this is possible).

So, ask them why they responded the way they did. What turned them on to you and your offer? To your product or service? Why you and not the competition? Why you at this time?

It's amazing what you can learn by asking. You might offer a small gift as a thank-you for their time in helping you, or you may not. In any case, ask and ye shall receive.

The other side of the coin is a tad harder. To get to the bottom of why what didn't work did not work could take a little more effort. The reason is you have no customers, or very few. If you did an offer or package or list test and you're dealing with the losing group, you have somewhere between a few and nil customers. It's tough to work with small numbers.

You can still do with the "did not work" group exactly what you did with the winners. Ask them questions as to "why not." It will take longer and will be more difficult, but it will work. You will have more turn-offs than helpful hints—yet when you're finished, you will know why what didn't work did not work.

What Are You Going to Do with This Knowledge Next Time?

Or, as Hewlett Packard asked in an advertising campaign of long ago: "What if . . ."

Computers are marvelous, aren't they? Without them, nothing in the business world would be the same—or even close to it. Direct response has been blessed by their use. Because of them we are more cost-efficient, effective, and selective.

With computers we have the capability to gather all sorts of data—in fact, tons of it—and then we don't use it! Our time is too valuable to waste. It doesn't make sense to gather information and ask questions, and then analyze the results on issues only remotely likely to occur. Or that aren't important, BIG issues in the first place.

You should plan to deal only with facts and the opportunities they offer that can make a difference. Every little detail will not make a difference. It is important, as you organize your program and think about measurement, to plan to save only the important stuff. Things you know will make a difference in your decisions and will help you build your database for future exploitation.

As you're doing this information gathering, make sure it is true and useful knowledge—not just facts and figures, numbers and words. Instead, it should be real knowledge about you, your products, and your services as your customers and prospects see them.

Make certain what you save after analysis is data that will be useful to you tomorrow, the next day, and the next. Not just "stuff" to keep the researchers happy. How do you know what to save? I don't know. Only with experience do you gain knowledge and decide what is truly important to you. In the beginning, it is guesswork and common sense.

Working with a high-tech company introducing a new product, we saved data on nearly 100 creative/media combinations. In less than 5 months, we knew which 20 were important and dumped the rest.

Years ago, I worked with a transportation company, dividing its large list into useful segments. In this case, the selections contacted were too finite; much of it was never used and most certainly was not cost-effective. This was a kill of a good idea, because the computer was available, the process was inexpensive, and the information was easy to pump. Not a good decision.

Don't dump anything too soon, unless you truly feel you'll never use it. Think about the elements, the BIG pieces, where a difference can be important. Save and store and massage and manipulate that information. Turn it into knowledge—something beneficial to be used later to increase your share and profits in the marketplace.

■ Direct Marketer's Basic Formulas ■

What are some of the important things you look for when analyzing your direct marketing program? And how do you measure if the program worked or not?

In addition to the ideas already given in this chapter, there are some formulas you might find helpful. Here are 5 I found useful as I looked at various campaigns to measure what happened.

Response Percentage
For direct mail:

> Response percentage = Orders received divided by pieces mailed
> (200 orders/10,000 mailing = 2% response)

For space ads:

> Response percentage = Orders received divided by circulation
> (200 orders/200,000 circulation = .1% response)

For TV/radio:

> Response percentage = Orders received divided by audience
> (200 orders/1,000,000 audience = .02% response)

Average Unit of Sale

Average unit of sale (AUS) = Total income divided by number of buyers
($20,000 income/200 buyers = $100 AUS)

Gross Profit

For direct mail:

Gross profit = Income minus mailing costs
($20,000 income − $7,500 cost = $12,500 gross profit)

For space ads:

Gross profit = Income minus ad placement costs
($20,000 income − $5,000 cost = $15,000 gross profit)

For TV/radio:

Gross profit = Income minus time charges
(creative charges are amortized over many promotions)
($20,000 income − $10,000 cost = $10,000 gross profit)

Cost per Sale

For direct mail:

Cost per sale = Mailing cost divided by number of sales
($7,500 cost/200 sales = $37.50 cost per sale)

For space ads:

Cost per sale = Space costs divided by number of sales
($5,000 cost/200 sales = $25 cost per sale)

For TV/radio:

Cost per sale = Time costs divided by number of sales
($10,000 cost/200 sales = $50 cost per sale)

Cost per Thousand

For direct mail:

Cost per thousand (CPM) = Mailing cost divided by pieces mailed × 1,000
($7,500 cost/10,000 mailers × 1,000 = $750 CPM)

For space ads:

> CPM = Space cost divided by circulation × 1,000
> ($5,000 cost/200,000 circulation × 1,000 = $25 CPM)

For TV/radio:

> CPM = Time cost divided by audience × 1,000
> ($10,000 cost/1,000,000 audience × 1,000 = $10 CPM)

▪ The Square Root of Wonderful ▪

And then there is another formula, the Square Root of Wonderful, which is a little different from the others.

Just because one list or offer pulls a few more responses than another doesn't always mean it is actually better. Remember, you're testing samples of a universe and measuring what happens. Analyzing to determine the next best step to take. Sometimes the difference between 2 lists is simply the sample size. Sometimes it is more complex, with one offer dramatically different than another. A price test is a good example—where you are measuring the effect on response of one price ($29.95), against another ($49.95).

There are all sorts of mathematical tables and formulas to figure all this out. Yet, if you're like me and had trouble with high school geometry and introductory algebra, you'll appreciate the Square Root of Wonderful. It goes like this:

> If the difference between 2 tests is greater than the square root of their total, the difference is statistically significant. And you should pay attention to that difference.

For example, package A gets 38 responses and package B gets 62 responses (B − A = 24). The square root of A + B = the square root of 100, or 10. Since 24 is greater than 10, the difference here is significant.

Now a different example, using the same formula. Package A gets 54 responses and package B gets 46 responses (A − B = 8). The square root of A + B = the square root of 100, or 10. The difference between these two packages is too close to call—they are statistically identical.

▪ HOW BIG IS A TEST? ▪

Let's have a little dialogue about how big a test should be. How large is large; how small is small? And what difference does it make?

Vin Jenkins, principal in his own direct response agency in Australia, has gone to great lengths to demonstrate that an honest and valid test of lists, an offer, a package—anything with direct mail—can be done with fewer than 2,000 units. If you do everything right and have the sophisticated math models necessary, I'm sure Vin is correct. It can work.

Another view is held by Al Mercer of Canada. Al talks about a 10% rule. This rule of thumb says you always test 10% of a list to predict how it is most likely to perform in a rollout. No matter the size of the list universe, you always test 10%.

And then, there is me. I more or less disagree with both of these fine, experienced direct marketing pros. Why? Because I sold lists for a number of years and have bought hundreds of lists for scores of clients since. I've been involved with direct response programs that used mail, space ads, telephone, fax, e-mail, the Web, and allied collateral and support materials. My comfort level is different because of my experience. It is different from both Vin's and Al's for testing lists, for testing offers of any type, for testing creative—for testing anything.

Why do list owners, managers, and brokers have minimum order numbers for lists? One reason is the volume required for computers to be cost-efficient. A more important reason is that *unless you put enough numbers into the marketplace, you will not have a measurable response to analyze.*

It is not uncommon for lists to be available in a minimum 5,000 or 10,000 quantity. The list owner or broker wants the list to work just as much as you do. Without a sufficient test, you may never be sure. Even if you hit it lucky and get a high response off a small number mailed, there is no assurance you'll experience the same results with the rollout.

Personally, I'm not comfortable with less than 2,500 names in any one test cell, especially in an offer test—a test of price, a premium, a limited time offer, anything. And I really prefer 5,000 names on all list tests as a minimum.

The key in testing, and the subsequent measurement and analysis of what happens, is not how many prospects hear, see, or read about you—it is how many respond! Response is the key, the trigger. Not the number out the door, the number that come back.

When you test direct mail packages, layout and design, different copy approaches, various package sizes, offers of any and all types, what you are seeking is a winning package. And, as the title of this chapter suggests, winning isn't everything, but who cares about all that other stuff?

Television and space ads are different because your audience reach is different. Here you're talking to thousands, maybe millions, with a single effort. With print and broadcast, you will get a feel of success quickly—maybe with one insertion of the ad or a short flight of broadcast. And you'll be able to analyze and decide direction.

Well, what's best for you? Beats me! Like a broken record, "I don't know" and "it depends" are still the correct answers. What you test and the size of the test, even *if* you test, very likely will be influenced, if not decided, by the size of your marketplace.

If you're a consumer marketer you probably have tens of thousands to millions of prospects. If you're business-to-business, you may have only a handful. You must decide what's best for you.

▪ Hindsight Is an Exact Science ▪

Analysis is the eighth point of The 8ight Point Market Action Plan. It wraps up the program. It comes at the end. It closes the loop. It brings you back to the beginning so you can start again. And even though it is last, it must be considered as you are developing your objectives, setting your budget and timetable, defining your audience, deciding your offer, and preparing the creative.

If you don't do it up front, when evaluation time rolls around you won't be ready. You won't have made the necessary decisions on what is important, what you are going to measure, what you will analyze.

Why analyze? In summary, you analyze the results of your direct response campaign to find out these things:

- Was this campaign, or program justified? Did it pay? (Remembering all the time that "PROFIT" is not a 4-letter word—you are supposed to make a profit.)
- Should we continue with this same program exactly as is, to the same audience, with the same offer, or should we make changes?
- How can we improve on the successes we have enjoyed thus far? How can we make this campaign better?

Power direct marketing works in a circle. You begin with objectives and work your way through to the end, analysis/measurement. Which really isn't the end at all. It is the beginning. The beginning of the next phase of your ongoing marketing campaign. By analyzing your results, you learn what really happened and feed that input back in at the top to start all over again. *This* is power direct marketing!

Chapter 10

THE END

PLANNING IS EVERYTHING—THE PLAN IS NOTHING

. . .

In the summer of 1772, a young man wrote Benjamin Franklin seeking executive and management advice. Franklin replied, "I cannot advise you *what* to determine, but if you please I will tell you *how*."

Power direct marketing works through The 8ight Point Market Action Plan, and The 8ight Point Plan is a "how" work tool. It is not designed to tell you what to do. In fact, some of you may feel you would be more comfortable with some specific "do this" and "don't do that" statements.

Direct response marketing doesn't lend itself, as a marketing discipline, to such rash, bold, black-and-white proclamations. Direct response is an art—it is not a science. Yes, there are rules, if you care to call them such. In reality, what we have is a set of experiences, built over time, that at best turn into guidelines. More accurately stated, they should simply be called IDEAS.

Whether they are rules or guidelines or ideas, they don't always work. Nothing always works! Even the best marketing planning isn't always going to do for you what you need most.

Planning is one of the basic functions of management. Direct marketing planning is a basic function of marketing management.

Whether you elect to be informal with your planning or more formal with a structure, you are taking a step with your company's future. You are getting ready for the marketplace.

Dick Dixon said it very well: " . . . planning simply means targeting your efforts on the future of your business."

Harry Lorayne says it another way: "Most problems precisely defined are already partially solved."

Planning IS everything!

■ DIRECT RESPONSE MARKETING: WHAT IS IT? WHAT CAN IT DO? ■

As mentioned earlier, direct marketing is NOT the adult phrase for direct mail. Yes, direct mail is still the mainstay of many direct response programs. Still, the two terms—direct marketing and direct mail—are not equal.

Direct marketing is the umbrella term for all that happens in direct response. Direct marketing makes use of most of the media available to other disciplines. These include both commercial and cable television; radio; magazines of every description—business and consumer, farm and general, vertical special interest; newspapers; the telephone; and direct mail. The most interesting of the "new" tools for direct marketing is the World Wide Web and its support buddy, e-mail. There are others, but these are the most frequently used tools of direct marketing.

Bottom-up marketing is what direct response marketing is all about. It is the opposite of mass marketing. It is reaching for specific audiences and specific segments of those audiences and making them a specific and direct offer.

Direct response marketing gets people to act now. Not everyone, just the people you want to separate from the mass market, the people who are your best prospects. Direct marketing is a carefully planned, precise tool that allows you to determine which approach, which offer, which format is best, and by how much.

Direct response marketing creates an immediate response on the part of prospects. They take action to inquire about or to acquire the product or service you are offering. Prospects may respond to a mailing piece; to a television commercial (with a toll-free number and/or address); by cutting a coupon or pop-up in a magazine, newspaper advertisement, or insert; by clicking the send button on your Web site; and, at the other end of the spectrum, by responding to an offer on a matchbook.

Direct response marketing can increase your profits in a number of different ways. It can help identify and segment your market, and make profitable use of your current customer names to build new sales in old markets and open up new markets for you.

For example, approximately 33% of all contributions to fund-raising organizations occur because of direct response, and 70% of all magazine subscriptions are sold through direct marketing techniques. More books are sold through direct response than in all the bookstores combined. More business-to-business leads are generated by direct response than by any other means.

▪ DEFINITIONS ▪

Let's do some definitions. In every case, these were learned from my dad, who said he never sold anything in his life. Maybe so, but he sure did buy a lot of stuff!

Advertising

Advertising does these 6 things, probably better than any other discipline:

- It *educates* a marketplace—your current customers and your best prospects.
- It *informs* the marketplace about a new product, a store opening, a sale, something.

- It makes the audience *aware* of a product or service they may not have known about.
- It creates an *image* of the product or service being offered.
- It *positions* the product or service in the market with similar and competitive brands.
- It generates *interest*, the goal being to get the prospects to move from where they are to making a purchasing decision.

Marketing

Now, let's define *marketing*—general marketing. Marketing is finding out and providing what your customers want.

Silicon Valley public relations expert Paul Franson says customers are demanding things be done their way—this is now the rule, not the exception. Marketing must understand this very real situation and address it head-on.

Selling

Selling is getting your prospect and customer to buy from YOU and not from someone else. Selling and marketing work hand in glove together.

The direction is clear. The greater selectivity available since the end of the Korean War in the 1950s has led from mass marketing to segmented marketing, then to niche marketing, and finally to one-on-one. Quite a change from the "everybody is a prospect" philosophy that prevailed at an earlier time.

Today, you talk to people as individuals. There was a time when mass made sense. There were fewer goods and fewer options. There were not 8 varieties of Coca Cola. In fact, there were not more than a handful of soft drink suppliers. Telephones came like the Ford Model T. You could have it any color you wanted, as long as that color was black.

Companies owned a category—not a brand, but an entire category. Not today. A while back a friend from New Zealand lived with us for several months. She was amazed at our variety of products. The country of New Zealand is about the size of California and has a population of just over 3.5 million people. The city of Los Angeles has more than 3 million people. So, it is easy to see and understand why we in North America can support a wide variety of products and services and New Zealand has to do with less. It was a great experience to take Erin to the supermarket and just watch her walk the aisles with scores of flavors, sizes, colors—dozens of options inside a single product group. So many choices. Things do change.

In the late 1950s, jets were put on airplanes. An 11-hour flight from the West Coast to Hawaii became only 5 hours. Your flight no longer had to stop during a trip from the East Coast to the West Coast. Transportation changed dramatically.

The 1960s were alive with action and activity. If you wanted to move, change jobs, get married, get divorced, tell off your boss, smoke pot—you did it. The "me" generation was active. If you were alive and even somewhat well, got up in the morning and showed up at your plant or office, you made a very nice living, thank you. All you had to do in the 1960s was exist to live. That all changed about 1969, and the world hasn't been the same since.

Lifestyles changed. Minorities were "discovered." The women who worked during and after World War II and the war in Korea were no longer satisfied with just jobs—they wanted and demanded careers.

A choice of brands was okay; a choice of products was better. Demographics were important; psychographics were more important. They both overlaid geographics, and it did make a difference.

Mass marketing became "not for me." "I'm someone" became the battle cry. "Treat me as such. Talk to me as a person, an individual. Different products and services for different niches. Address my specific needs." As audiences became fragmented, they also became more knowledgeable—the marketplace got smart.

One of the key reasons this all happened is what is commonly called the Information Age or Explosion. Information is fine; I prefer

Table 10.1 ■ The Knowledge Ladder

Years	Information Factor
To 1900	1
1900–1950	2
1950–1975	64
1975–1990	2×2
1990–2000	2×1
By 2020	?

to talk about *knowledge*. Information that becomes useful is knowledge to the consumer, to the marketplace.

What has happened is this (See Table 10.1). If we took all the recorded information from the beginning of time through the year 1900 and factored it, the number would be 1. This is approximately 6,000 years of recorded history. Between 1900 and 1950, that information doubled. So the number is now 2. Between 1950 and 1975, it doubled every 5 years, making the new number 64. From 1975 to 1990, available knowledge doubled every 2 years. By the year 2000, it was doubling at a rate of once every year. And by 2020? The predication is it will double every 35 days!

Look what else is forecast for the future, a future most of us will be around for. It is predicted that by the year 2020, 97% of the information we will know and use doesn't exist yet. Wow!

Who's driving the marketing revolution? Customers and prospects are driving it! They have NEEDS, and know there is a place for those needs to be fulfilled. Those companies that are most acutely aware of this revolution can readily see why the capabilities of direct response marketing are right for today's marketplace. These companies will embrace direct response as a prime force for growth and success.

One company that understands the marketing revolution and is doing something about it is the Marriott Corporation. Today, it offers a brand umbrella of the Marriott name and 7 hotel concepts to appeal to 7 different market niches:

- **Marriott Marquis**—For major markets, large hotels with convention capabilities
- **Marriott Resorts**—For vacations and smaller conventions
- **Marriott Suite**—Targeted at the upscale suite audience
- **Marriott**—Aimed at the regular business traveler and meeting planner with small group needs
- **Residence Inns**—The only one in the group without Marriott in the name—reaching for executives who need a moderate suite for a number of days
- **Marriott Courtyard**—Looking for the upper end of the mid-priced market
- **Marriott Fairfield**—The opposite of Courtyard, segmenting to the traveler on a limited budget

This is really identifying, dividing, and conquering the marketplace! Gerald A. Michaelson said it well: "Segment! Or you will be segmented."

■ THE 11 ADVANTAGES OF DIRECT RESPONSE MARKETING ■

Let's lay the foundation for direct response with these thoughts—11 advantages, 11 reasons it works.

Action

Direct response is an ACTION medium. It invites response. It encourages it. It almost *demands* attention. You're supposed to DO something, take some action.

It is not a passive medium. It is more than general advertising, more than information and education. More than awareness, position, and image building. You are to call the toll-free number. Mail the response card. Click the box on the Web page. Visit the trade show. Complete the order form. Return the faxback form. Direct response is an action, a "do" tool.

Measurable

Direct response is MEASURABLE. Because it is action oriented, it is measurable. You can count the reply cards and the coupons. The number of inbound calls received asking for your FREE offer or other information. Or the number requesting to see a sales rep for a live demonstration.

How many purchase orders came in today's mail or by e-mail? How many checks and credit card orders were received? Unlike other media, which rely on estimated reach and frequency figures, you know *exactly* what happened. You know where your leads and orders came from, and you know the cost.

Flexible

Direct response is FLEXIBLE. It can serve as a support tool with general advertising and/or public relations. It can be part of a sales promotion program. Or, it can go it alone as the only technique used. It can be the channel of distribution, a mail-order medium, or a way to generate leads or to build traffic.

Versatile

Direct response is VERSATILE. You can do many things with it. Send a basic letter/envelope/reply card format, a catalog, a 3-D package. There's almost no limit to the size, shape, format, content, or design of your direct mail. (There are some post office regulations, which you'll do well to become familiar with, but you have lots of leeway.)

There are few creative bounds to your print/space program or television campaign. Only your imagination limits what you might dream up for your Web site. And you can vary your message and method of distribution to suit your timing, audience segments, offer, objectives, and budget.

Selective

Direct response is a SELECTIVE target medium. Not so mass marketing, where the measure is numbers alone. With direct response you are very specific, selecting the best list for mail and phone marketing, the vertical or special-interest magazine, newspaper, newsletter. Even broadcast and Web pages have "direction" by how they are marketed, the audience to whom they are directed.

Direct response is discriminating. It is not random, but targeted. It allows and encourages response from groups that have been most carefully selected.

Personal

Direct response is PERSONAL. The most pleasing sound known to people is the sound of their own name. A name gives identity, a sense of being—especially with direct mail and the telephone, which allow for personal contact with your audiences. Direct marketing is personal.

Direct marketing encourages personalization not available with any other medium. You can communicate with each individual in your carefully targeted group and talk to him or her by name.

Confidential

Direct response is CONFIDENTIAL. Only you know who you have selected from your telephone or mailing list. It's not easy for your competition to know what you're up to. You can make your message personal, one-on-one to your best prospects and customers. Direct mail, e-mail, faxes, and the telephone allow this intimacy.

Persuasive

Direct response is PERSUASIVE. Persuasion is a sales word. Marketing is selling to your audience, so to be effective, direct response must be persuasive.

When you use direct response marketing techniques, you are putting marketing and sales together, working as a team. To convince your target group what you have to offer is what they need to fulfill their needs. And to prove now is the time to take action.

Economical

Direct response is ECONOMICAL. It is cost-effective because you select and talk only to those most likely to respond, to buy what you are offering. There is very little waste because you target, using direct mail, e-mail, vertical print, fax, and telephone. Your message is being received by those most likely to be interested in what you have to say.

Testing

Direct response is a TESTING tool. It allows you to test mailing lists against each other and against offers. It allows you to test offers against each other and mailing lists. Offers also can be tested in print or with telemarketing or on television or through the Web and e-mail.

The response rates from each segment of each test can be measured statistically to aid you in your decision making, in getting to the best bottom line. In determining which audience, which offer, which package will earn you the best results.

Effective

Direct response is EFFECTIVE. It is effective because it is a sales tool! Direct response is designed to get a lead, an order—to build traffic. It either gets a sale itself, as in mail order, or it leads to the sale, as in lead generation.

Mail order business-to-business is big business today. Most business books, tapes, and other training aids are sold using direct response marketing techniques. Office and computer supplies are effectively, efficiently, and profitably sold through direct response.

Direct response techniques are also used effectively for lead generation for both consumer and business programs. A considerable sum is totaled each year by fund-raisers using direct mail, the press, broadcast, and the telephone. Many local and national, small and large companies with storefronts use direct marketing to build traffic through their doors.

Through all direct response there is a common thread, a single denominator, no matter what your product, your service, or the tools you use: AFTO. Asking for the order is what makes it effective. When you use direct mail, print, phone, collateral, sales materials, radio and television, and the Web—solo or in combination—in direct response, there is always an AFTO. Which is why it works, why it is effective!

▪ The Planning Model ▪

The one thing we can be absolutely sure of is that the future will be distinctly different from the past. The world of the future—even a few years ahead to 2020, as we talked about earlier—will be different from today.

As difficult as it may seem, if we are to be as successful with our businesses as we know we can be, we must plan for that future. We must consider the impact it will have on our businesses and be prepared to take steps to change our operation to get in step with the times as they change.

An important benefit of planning is that you are in a position to take advantage of change, to be able to move with the times. To observe the marketplace and then the advantage of that new opportunity or changed situation.

Dale Marco of Peat, Marwick, Mitchell & Co. said it well: "Planning is deciding in the present what to do in the future."

Many senior executives (middle managers, too) tend to be action oriented. They prefer doing something—sometimes anything other than planning what to do. The planning process takes time, and the feeling is there isn't time. How can we set aside planning time?

The Koran says: "If you don't know where you are going, any road will take you there." We all know that is true, so why do we resist planning? How can we possibly know where we're going if we don't have a plan to take us there?

Clarence Eldridge of the Campbell Soup Company has a response:

> Writing a marketing plan sounds like quite a chore to do once a year on every product. It is quite a chore—the first time. Thereafter . . . the practice saves rather than consumes time.
>
> It provides the necessity for complete basic agreement at the beginning of the year, with respect to the job to be done and the way to go about doing it. It permits making reasonably long-range plans to which the company is broadly committed, and obviates the likelihood of costly improvisation and changing of direction.
>
> It provides, better than any other system I know, for that continuity of effort and of direction that is so important to the successful working out of any marketing activities.

Figure 10.1 ■ The 8ight Point Market Action Plan

The 8ight Point Market Action Plan is my answer to those who don't have time. To those who don't have a plan and know they need one. Nobody argues against the concept of planning. They may only argue against the technique or process. For these people, The 8ight Point Plan is my answer (see Figure 10.1). It is simple, easy to understand, quick to follow. Not a formula, just guidelines and IDEAS.

One last time, let's walk through the 8 steps of this action planning process one by one. Let's summarize the meaning and benefits of each point.

Objectives

Do have a mission, a goal, a stated focus and direction. Begin the plan with a simple summary of what business you are in and what you plan to achieve over the coming year or with this campaign, effort, or program.

Include specifics that can be measurable. Real, live numbers you plan on meeting or exceeding. Pinpoint your objectives. The real tragedy of any program is not in not reaching your goal. The real tragedy is in having no goal to reach.

Ask questions to firm up your objectives: What market share do you want—how much? What increase do you expect—how much? And where? In what markets? From which consumers? Have specific, measurable objectives, and you'll be well on your way to success.

Be tough with your objectives, realistic. IBM is one of the better companies at setting objectives with all its sales teams. One by one each year, for each product line, it sets realistic objectives. Each sales rep has a different set of goals. Based on that rep's experience, the territory, and the product line, the objectives are set.

Your objectives also must fit—be compatible—with the other activities of your organization. If they are not, you may soon have a major in-house problem. Possibly even a true disaster.

The last couple of decades of the 20th century have given us scores of examples of "new," with true space age products being dreamt up, designed, built, and brought to market.

One of the more exciting stories is the National Aeronautic and Space Administration (NASA) sending a mission to Mars with less time and less money than any proposal ever imagined. Yet, the team pulled together to reach this objective and did it. They did it on time and under budget. How? They had a plan with few rules and lots of innovative thinking. NASA didn't just "change,"—they also CHARGED!

Most of us have heard the Apple Computer story of the 1980s. They too gave themselves a year to reach an out of sight (for the time) objective to break into the PC market. It worked for Apple, too. The story became famous in the Santa Clara Valley of California because, among other things, they had a 24-hour-a-day work schedule and a video game room as a "standard" part of their operation. Different, certainly not compatible with most business practices. Yet, at the end of the year that new computer was built. They achieved their objective because they had a plan. They too, ahead of their time, CHARGED!

All objectives must be reached with a set time frame. You must have a schedule to reach your objectives. Rarely do you book too much time. Usually it's the other way 'round—you fail to allow sufficient time. In any case, include timing as part of setting objectives.

Although I've never worked on any direct marketing program where we didn't have at least some of the direction in writing, I do know of marketers who wing it. They are the type of people who say, "So, you've got a problem? Here's the answer. Got another problem? Here's another answer. Nobody reads all that stuff anyway. And besides, putting it in writing takes away time from real work."

Sound familiar? If that is what happens in your company—you play the game by the seat-of-the-pants response method—you are less likely to have good objectives. And even less likely to achieve much of anything.

Another reason you put your objectives in writing is so you'll have something to change. As Katie Muldoon, president of her own direct response agency, says:

> Be prepared to revise your marketing plan as time goes on. Review it, both in terms of overall policy and the numbers you came up with originally. Review your image and your product mix. Often we become so busy with day-to-day running of our business we forget to step back and ask ourselves, "Are we on track?"

When your objectives are in writing, it is easier to do what Katie suggests.

Timetable

The next step in The 8ight Point Plan is Timetable. Having a timetable involves 2 activities:

1. A schedule to implement your direct marketing program or campaign
2. The best time to use direct response for your product or service

You must have a time frame to achieve the objectives you've set. If you don't set a time to reach your goals, guess what? You're much less likely to arrive anywhere!

The same reason limited time offers work to get people to take action applies to having a time frame to reach your corporate or program objectives. We as people tend to procrastinate. Are you caught up with your business reading? That stack of night and weekend reading material? Why not? One of the reasons has to be there is a lack of urgency to it, so you just put it off. You can't do that with your direct marketing plan.

Professor Thomas W. Bonoma said it best: "You can't know if your plan is any good if it is not executed."

The second reason you have a timetable is to plan what season to be in the marketplace, to decide the best timing to reach your best prospects and key customers. For many products and services, timing is a nonissue. An example is telephone products. Any time is a good time—they move year-round. For others, timing is important. They are big movers only at select times of the year. Christmas trees in July are a tough sell—between the end of November and Christmas Eve you'll do just fine.

Sometimes we make more out of a season than it deserves. Businesses make buying decisions every day. You and I at home make buying decisions several times each month.

Consideration of when to introduce your new product, have a special product line sale, or do a lead generation program for your sales staff can be totally up to you. On the other hand, a fund-raising drive for a special disaster relief project, or an invitation to your customers and best prospects to a trade show you are exhibiting in, will be dictated by outside forces. Sometimes the timing is picked for you.

When you have total control, you may look at market trends in your industry or evaluate competitive activity. You may decide the first half of the month or the last third of the quarter is best.

There is no right or wrong with setting a timetable. There is only a "do"—you must do it.

Budget

Budget is the third point of The 8ight Point Plan. Accounting sees direct marketing as an expense. Top management views it as an investment. For the marketing team, it's the lifeblood of the organization—

it's the effort that keeps the phones ringing, the sales team singing, and the factory humming. And it's never big enough!

Of course, "it" is the budget. When you've been in marketing for 1 day, you've experienced a budget because you can't operate without one. Money—in whatever form you get and use it—is a necessity.

There is a multitude of ways to set a budget for your campaign. Many in direct response prefer to work on a project-by-project basis, with what is called the "task" method of budgeting. It is popular because you assign what is necessary to accomplish your agreed-on objectives within the time frame allowed. Sometimes this is not only the easiest way to calculate your budget, it is the most efficient and effective, because you are working with a known situation on a project basis.

Using an arbitrary formula or estimating based on what happened last year or from raw industry statistics is also easy. Unfortunately, easily developed budgets also tend to be poor performers. You spend too much—or not enough—or worse yet, you don't know if it's right or wrong.

Budgets need to be planned, just like everything else in direct response. Here are some things to look for as you plan your budget:

▪ Start with specific objectives. Deal with projected figures rather than ancient history—last year's performance doesn't tell you enough. Aim for real numbers, not X% of something or other. Remember, direct response must be measurable if you're to improve your program and know where you're growing.

▪ Look at the competition. If for no other reason than to know where you stand in comparison. If your objectives include some goals that relate to market share or overtaking another position in the standings, you need to know what is going on in the marketplace.

This does not mean a small company can always do big things. It does mean if you're going to play with the big boys, you have to act like the big boys. By knowing what's happening, you can plan where to be with your budget for the most effective results.

■ Know where you are in your direct marketing cycle. Are you a well-established company? Is your product established or new? If you're launching anything new, it will take more than if you're in a maintenance mode. Is this a prime promotional time or a quiet period? Know where you are. It will affect your budget.

■ Know what portion of the marketing message will be carried by marketing and what share by sales. Sometimes marketing is NOT the answer. Sometimes something else will be better. Advertising, public relations, or sales promotion may be needed to create awareness, set the image, position the product. It could be this time marketing will play a secondary role. Know the marketing responsibility.

■ Get 'em while they're hot! Build budget flexibility into your plan to allow you to react to a situation. Be prepared to speed up the use of funds if required to take advantage of an unusual opportunity.

■ Allow enough money for an ongoing campaign. Those companies that float in and out of the marketplace show inconsistency not only with their programs but also to their customers and prospects. Even though it is not always so, you don't look as stable as if you're always visible. Plan your program to be around when your customer is ready to buy.

Just as you need to plan your budget, you also need to make a firm commitment to the budget. Make a commitment that says you're going to support direct marketing, its objectives, and planned programs.

Audience

Audience is the next step of The 8ight Point Market Action Plan—and the most important.

Larry Lamattina, an advertising executive from New York, made an interesting prediction late in the 1980s: "In the year 2010 many more media vehicles will be used. The end result will be more fragmented, but far more targeted." BINGO!

Where has this advertising professional been? From at least the early 1970s direct marketing has known the advantages of a more fragmented, but far more targeted audience.

No matter how great your promotion—your sharp direct mail, your 4-color coupon ad, your slick television commercial—it won't do well if it goes to the wrong people. Getting your message to the right audience is *the* key element in direct response marketing. If you do all else only so-so, yet target the right audience, you have an excellent chance of turning up a winner.

The single most important part of audience is identifying customers' interest, determining what is most interesting. Offers are not good or bad, creative is not short or long—everything can be reduced to simply interesting or uninteresting.

Here are 6 ideas about selecting the right audience for your message:

▪ *Redefine your market before you begin the creative process.* Get the most current demographic, psychographic, and geographic information available. If you're in business marketing, identify the proper Standard Industrial Classification (SIC) codes and the correct job titles.

▪ *Redefine your product or service and how it fits with each of your markets.* Make certain you know what you're selling, understand what your offer is. If you're not up on the product, talk to those who are. Know as much as you can before you start to create. Know your audience and their wants, desires, and needs.

▪ *Talk to your current buyers. Know what they know.* Find out from them what they think of you. What are your strengths and weaknesses? Does your audience know? Do they care? Talk to your customers.

▪ *Redefine your prospect sources based on what you learn from your buyers.* If geography is a factor, find those prospects closest to your current customers. Know you probably will have to Ask for the Order several times before receiving it.

■ *Fit your service or product to your marketplace.* Prepare your creative to fit your audience. Talk to them in their language. Choose the right words for direct mail, print, the Web, broadcast, and telephone options.

■ *Sell the benefits and advantages, address needs, express understanding— be interesting to your audience.* The sizzle still moves as many people to take action as the steak. Make certain your audience know WII-FM— What's In It For Me.

Direct mail is still the major tool of direct response. Selecting the right list—getting to the preferred audience—is mandatory for success. Here is a laundry list of ideas lifted and revised from Citibank/Australia, things to look for when you rent a list for your use. They are the questions to get answers to before making a list purchasing decision:

1. What type of list is it—customers, inquiries, compiled, response, active, or inactive?
2. Personal data—what demographic and psychographic information is available?
3. Transaction data—do you know whether this audience has been active recently, with what frequency, and for what dollar amount? Use the classic recency/frequency/ monetary (RFM) formula.
4. What medium was used to acquire the names in the first place—direct mail, space, broadcast, the Web, a trade show, consumer sweeps, or something else?
5. What is the size of the list—the universe—and the minimum quantity to test?
6. In what sequence is the list available—postal code, alpha order, how else?
7. In what format is it available—disk, cheshire or peel-off labels, magnetic tape?
8. What form of key coding is available—what options do you have to code for measurement?

9. How often is the list cleaned and updated?
10. What method of random sample selection is available?
11. How often has this list been used in the last 12 months? What was the last date of usage, who has used it most, and what have the results been?
12. Does the list owner require a sample of your direct mail package prior to mailing?
13. How much does it cost—what is the rental rate, test rate, repeat order rate, and selection surcharge?

As you're putting your direct mail program together, this checklist should prove useful if you will be purchasing outside mailing lists.

No matter the tools you use—mail, print, broadcast, fax, telephone, or e-mail—your audience is still your most important element. Select it carefully.

Offer

If a man can write a better book, preach a better sermon, or make a better mousetrap than his neighbor, though he builds his house in the woods, the world will make a beaten path to his door.

Ralph Waldo Emerson

The fifth point of The 8ight Point Plan is Offer. Your offer is next in importance to audience as you plan your direct response marketing program. The quote from Mr. Emerson may have been true in his day, but it certainly is not today! Just because you have a product or service offering benefits to your select audience, it does not mean anyone will even think about you, let alone beat a path to your door. Which is why an offer is so important in direct response.

The purpose of an offer is to get that special audience to stop, look, listen, and understand your offer is for them. And they should take advantage of the opportunity and place an order—with you. Now!

How do you put a good offer together? What makes a good offer? Here are 17 ideas or ways to present your message to get that audience to STOP and consider you:

- Free information, a booklet, or literature
- Free gift or premium, tied to an order, a product demonstration, or a lead program
- A bonus for quick reply or cash with order
- Yes/no/maybe involvement devices to get your audience to do something
- Free product trial opportunity
- Discount price for response within a limited time
- Product guarantee or guarantee of satisfaction
- A contest, sweepstakes, or other "game"
- A limited time offer with a bonus, gift, or premium
- Friend-get-a-friend bonus offer program
- Negative option (their order continues to be fulfilled unless they say no)
- 'til forbid (their order continues to be fulfilled without them doing anything)
- Stamps, stickers, coupons, pop-ups, cut-outs, tear-offs, and perforations to gain more involvement
- Free sample of your product
- Charter "membership" in your organization or for a new publication
- Testimonials to the service you provide
- Case history stories to support your product applications

There are many more offer ideas. This list will get you thinking about the best way to present to your audience.

A word about business versus consumer. Yes, they are different, BUT you are still talking to people. People make decisions, not companies. And for the most part, the same good offers that work to you and me at home will work equally well to us at the office.

As you plan your program and consider the best offer to make, give every idea equal weight. Then decide, after some common sense evaluation, what will work best to your audience.

Maybe one of these next 7 ideas will work for you. Many times, we're dealing in everyday items, commodities, possibly with a mature product or service. How can you make an offer that will get your audience to pay some attention to you, to even consider what you have? Try one of these ideas.

Upgrade

Upgrade your product and make the upgrade the offer. Take your basic product, add to it, improve it, give it value.

That's why a gold credit card is worth more than a green card and the platinum more than the gold. That's why designer jeans cost more than "regular" jeans. In many cases a luxury automobile is not much more than fancy trim, more comfortable seats, and more buttons to push.

Downgrade

Downgrade—take away from what has always been. If status, image, polish, and position have been your trademark, remove some of the brass and offer less. Computer marketers have found they have a type of customer who wants only the basics, nothing more. They offer that (with clone products) and keep more of the marketplace.

Generic almost-everything is an example of downgrade. The products cross all categories, from cigarettes to medical supplies and drugs. Even Rolls Royce has a "downgrade" model—the Bentley.

Bundle

Bundle a group of your products or services that go together and sell them that way—as a group, in a bundle. As a package. The telephone companies have been excellent at doing this, packaging office products and services together and offering them at a special price.

The computer hardware manufacturers have gotten together with software geniuses and offered a bundle to the marketplace. A nice package for much of their market.

Unbundle

Unbundling is the flip side of bundling. If you already have a package, divide it and offer the parts. Allow your audience to pick and choose only what they really want.

The entire financial industry offers a variety of products you can buy in pieces. Life and health insurance companies and banks are examples. The discount brokerage house is probably the best example—its unbundled service being the offer.

Narrowcast

When your audience is huge and your competition numerous, you might find it beneficial to select a smaller group from the total or narrowcast. Work with a niche of the market, specializing in a "narrow" part. Do what direct response does best; concentrate your offer on that segment you can serve best.

Mass Market

Mass market is the opposite of narrowcast. You have been successful within a niche. You now take your idea, your success, your offer to a broader base. This concept has worked many times when an industrial product has found a spot in the much larger consumer marketplace. Many of the cleaning supplies in our homes today originally were found in factories.

A host of the 3M Corporation's 65,000 products began their commercial lives in offices around the world and now are everyday items in our homes. Scotch tape is the most notable example.

Price

Price is an offer consideration. In every survey as to the most important factors when a buying decision is made, price is there. Always in the top 10—many times in the top 5, NEVER in the top spot. Important, but not most important.

Here are 5 ways you can compete on price:

1. Offer more real *or* perceived value at a higher price.
2. Offer more value for the same price.

3. Offer the same value at a lower price.
4. Offer less value at a lower price.
5. Offer less value at a higher price.

Yes, each of these options can work. It all depends on you, your product, your competition, and your marketplace. Do not toss away any idea until you consider what it can do for you.

As you think about how to present your offer to your audience, look at the preceding ideas. See if 1 (or a combination of 2 or more) of them might work well for you and your audience.

Creative

Creative is the tactics of direct response. It is what you do to implement the strategy. It is putting your plan to work. Creative is the sixth point in The 8ight Point Plan. Until you have the first 5 points in order—Objectives, Timetable, Budget, Audience, Offer—you cannot do the creative.

You cannot begin your creative process until you know where you're going and what the purpose of the program is. And before you know that, you must have the first 5 points of the 8 in order. (Yes, sometimes the specific offer falls from the creative efforts. Yet, even in those cases, there is some general thought and direction as to what the offer might be.)

While many times we look for creative work that is very different, unusual, and innovative, sometimes it is better to be safe and stay with the known. And sometimes it is not!

The best creative work isn't necessarily that which appeals to you. Instead, it must appeal to your audience—your customers and prospects. It must meet their needs with a message in both copy and art that offers a benefit of doing business with you.

The best creative work is that which meets this short list of criteria:

- It stops your audience; it is noticed.
- If it is direct mail or e-mail, it is opened—now!

- If it is mail, e-mail, fax, or print it is read—now. If it is broadcast or telephone, it is listened to.
- The message is easy to understand; your audience knows what is expected and how they'll benefit.
- There is a reason to act now; there is an offer.
- And then AFTO. Always Ask for the Order, and do it more than once. Your audience, your prospect, your customer may not have heard you the first time you AFTO.

Some good friends from Ogilvy & Mather Direct in southeast Asia prepared a list of IDEAS to make your creative development work better, to help you evaluate the direct response work you prepare. Let me share my version of these thoughts with you:

1. Is your direct mail package, space ad, Web site, or television commercial designed so your specific objectives are likely to be met? From the beginning, do you know what your program is to achieve? Do your message, creative approach, and offer all work together to meet your objectives?

2. Is your direct marketing program—its presentation, copy, look, and feel—consistent with your overall company and product positioning? Does the creative complement you; does it fit your image in the marketplace?

3. Is your direct response program working synergistically with your public relations, sales promotion, and advertising? Do all of your communication efforts look like they were planned? Are they working together as a team?

4. Is your product or service offered in terms of the benefits your audience will gain by doing business with you? Are the features translated to benefits your reader or listener will understand?

5. Is your offer clearly, cleanly, and distinctly stated? Is your best offer listed first? Does your audience know what they will earn, learn, get, receive, win, or buy when they respond to your offer?

6. Is your coupon, business reply card, order form, ticket, or response device a standout piece? Does your audience automatically see this element in your mail, print, and e-mail and gravitate toward it?

7. Is this response device simple to understand and easy to read? Does it tell customers what to do, when, where, and how to do it? Is it easy to follow and to use? Is it easy to respond to your offer?

8. Does the headline in your ad and the teaser copy on direct mail encourage your customers or prospects to read more? To dig into the body copy and find out all they can? To get the complete message?

9. Does your entire direct mail package or space ad go together? Do all the pieces of the direct mail fit, 1 piece with another? Are the outer envelope, the letter, the brochure, and the response piece a compatible unit?

In your print advertisement, does the headline, subhead, and body copy carry your message? Do the layout and design, the graphics, all fit together as a unit and get your audience to the phone or fax number, the coupon, or the order card? Does it all feel right?

10. Do the graphics support the copy? Are they outstanding, attention-getting, yet not overwhelming? (Remember, copy is king in direct response. The sales message, the action is with the words.) Do the graphics encourage your audience to read the words?

The Creative Team

The care and feeding of creative people can be a humbling experience. Ego plays a large role in the creative process, and copywriters and art directors are no exceptions to its power.

To avoid much of the trauma that can go with preparing the best creative product, here are some ideas that will help you communicate:

- Care about the creative team as people. They are, you know. They are skilled at their trade. Communicate with them as individuals.
- Take enough time for a thorough briefing and put it in writing. Then talk about it. Both are important. Discuss the assignment with the copywriter and art director as a team—all of you working together as a team.

■ Include the creative team in everything. And tell them EVERYTHING. There is no such thing as too much knowledge. Let them decide what meetings they want to come to and what to do with those stacks of reports you dumped on their desks. Keep them fully informed about your product, the company, the competition, the marketplace. Tell them the no-nos they must know. Keep them on the same wavelength.

■ Challenge them. Ask questions every day about everything, including asking how you can help. Be receptive. Make sure you understand what they are doing and why.

■ Never flaunt your knowledge—share it. And make 110% certain all is understood. The direction is agreed on. The deadlines are real. The budget is set. Make sure you know what is going on daily. It is your responsibility to keep the train on the track, too.

■ Heap on praise, tons of praise. It is impossible to praise too much. Take credit for nothing; give it all away. Tell the creative team how much you appreciate what they have done to make this marketing program a winner. Then shut up and listen. It is amazing what you will learn.

■ As you listen, REACT. Don't just sit there, say something. Do something. Jump up. Sit down. Fight, fight, fight! Respond. Question. SCREAM. Be enthusiastic. Challenge again. Even doubt. Throw something. Hug somebody.

■ Allow the freedom to fail. Only with the freedom to fail do we have the freedom to succeed!

■ Criticize. Critique. Be active in the process of getting the best possible creative effort. Tell the creative team what you think and why. Is it good/bad/great/worse? Is it off strategy/unclear? Do you LOVE it? Tell them so they know. Share your thoughts and feelings.

■ Have fun. Few great things have been achieved in this world in an atmosphere of gloom and doom. Smile. Laugh. Cry if it helps. Enjoy. Work with the creative team and let them know it is a grand experience. When you do, your direct response campaign will be the best possible.

Production/Media

Production—doing the program, implementing the project, buying the space, arranging the printing and mailing—the "do" part of direct response is the seventh point in The 8ight Point Market Action Plan.

Friend Pat Haag of Creative Mailings has put together a list titled

9 Rules to Make Sure Your Direct Response Program Is Late, Wrong, and Over Budget!

As she says, "Followed diligently, you are guaranteed to delay, foul up, and increase your costs." Being positive by nature, I've accepted these rules from Pat, revised them with some ideas of my own, and present them here for you.

1. *Never become familiar with your suppliers' equipment and capabilities. Don't visit your printer, the letter shop, the telemarketing agency—work in a vacuum.*

Not knowing the length and breadth of the capabilities of those you're working with will, if nothing else, cause you to lose valuable time, and probably money.

Ask questions. Do find out what your suppliers can and cannot do. Determine whether you should go elsewhere for the job or split the assignment between 2 or more houses. You can only make those decisions if you know what is available in your marketplace. Find out ahead of time.

2. *Never, ever share with your suppliers more about the project than that portion which they are to perform. If you do tell your suppliers what you are really looking for, your desired end result, they just may be able to suggest another and better way to accomplish it for you.*

This may be the first time you've done this particular type of project. Undoubtedly your printer, letter shop, or agency has done something similar scores of times before. Ask them to help you. Share what you want and they may save you money or time—or both.

3. *No matter how many changes you made in a project, or how close to the due date you made them, never give your suppliers more time to produce a quality job.*

We all know due dates are sacred. However, we also know that many times due dates are pure fantasy, or artificial, not real. You're begging for mistakes by giving your suppliers too short a time to do an adequate job, no matter the assignment.

Remember, it's not their fault you (or someone) changed your mind half a dozen times. Making corrections is one thing; making changes is another. I've learned over time to question whether the change is really necessary. Sometimes when more money is involved or the due date will truly be missed because of changes, those changes have a way of becoming less important. And, if they really are needed, a little more money or a little more time to do them right is rarely a problem.

4. *Always design your direct mail packages with window envelopes that are too small for personalization. Never check to be certain all the pieces fit in the outgoing mailing envelope, nor the response device in the return envelope.*

Bless art directors, without them our world would be much less colorful and not nearly as interesting. However, in direct response, we must all remember we're in a dialogue business; you want the mail to be delivered and you want the reply to come back.

Direct mail packages must be designed to go together, to fit both outbound and incoming communication. Because personalization is so important in direct mail (if you have the correct name you should use it, it increases response!), your package must consider the mechanical elements.

How much space is needed to be certain everything fits? How much space do you need for the personalized letter or reply form to show through the window? Find out before you begin final art.

5. *Never plan ahead and allow for special paper needs or unique or different folds, cuts, or trims.*

When designing a personalized direct mail letter, a fancy fulfillment package brochure, something that will require an unusual paper, a different type of fold, a perforation, a pop-up, or other involvement device, you must tell your suppliers ahead of time. These extra nice action pieces take extra time to arrange and handle.

6. *Never consider international as requiring anything special or difficult.*
In direct mail the "standard" U.S. Post Office envelopes may not be accepted in other countries. You must think of this beforehand, and if you have a large number of customers or prospects overseas, make the necessary production arrangements.

The same for print advertising, television, and video standards—they are different in different parts of the world. You must know what they are if you are to operate successfully internationally.

7. *Never ask for counts by code from data processing before placing your order and printing.*
Measurability is a standard in direct response. When mailing numerous tests, you require numerous codes—so you can count and measure what happens. To save time afterward and money up front, get a count for each code before production.

By asking ahead of time, you can determine exactly what you need before personalizing with an incorrect tape or list, or before printing is done using incorrect quantities. If you're planning to include a tip-in response card on your space ad and want different codes for different publications, also be sure to plan ahead.

8. *Never ask for "live" samples when running personalized pieces until after the job is complete.*
"Live" samples of each direct mail test cell enable you to check your codes against your plan. They allow you to check for data processing, folding, and insertion errors. And to catch them before it's too late.

It does take extra time and a little more money to review and approve at this stage—and it's worth it!

9. *Never, never consider postage in your plans.*
The post office only takes money up front. You must pay before you mail. Those are the rules. Which means you must schedule payment prior to your mail date, either directly to the post office or to your mailing house.

If you're using a postage meter, it must be filled ahead of the lettershop processes. If you're using stamps, they must be purchased in advance, usually 3 to 5 days prior to the mail date.

Plan ahead—don't forget postage.

Analysis/Measurement

The eighth point of The 8ight Point Market Action Plan is analyzing and measuring your direct response program, determining how successful it was in the marketplace. Direct response marketing is the most measurable discipline you can employ if you want to really know what happened. If you want to track exactly your response, how many orders were received, how many leads generated, how many visits were made to your Web page, how many donations were made, or the foot traffic at your store or trade show booth.

As Steve Bedowitz of Amre, a company working in the fast-growth remodeling marketplace, says, "What I'm looking for is not the least expensive lead. I'm looking for the least expensive sale!" With direct marketing, Steve, and you, can know what is your least expensive sale.

If you want to know what it cost to talk to each prospect and convert each to a customer, direct response is the way to go. If you want to know your success rate in upgrading your customer base, use direct response. If you want to introduce a new product to a select marketplace, use direct response. In every case, you'll know what happened.

In a strange sort of way, the back end of direct marketing—the analysis and measurement stage—is just the beginning. With the knowledge you gain you can improve your marketing efforts. Because you learn not only how many orders you obtained, but the value of sales of those orders. Not just the number of leads, but how many were bought and for how much. Not just the store traffic you generate, but how many prospects become ongoing customers. Not only hits to your Web site, but also how many asked for literature and converted to customers. All because you count, you measure and analyze your results.

Another benefit of measurement is learning when your response really comes—the timing—and how it comes (phone, fax, mail, e-mail, walk-in, etc.).

Let's build a program to show some possibilities. You do a direct mailing that invites your audience to return the response card for more information on your offer, or to call a toll-free number or return the faxback form. Whichever is most convenient for them. This is a very common occurrence in both consumer and business promotions.

How will the split between mail and phone fall? Again, it depends on many factors. Is this a customer base or prospect mailing? Are you a known player in this field or an unknown? Is the product or service new or established? How much does it cost? What is the offer?

For this example, let's guess the direct mail will generate 30% of the total response, the fax another 30%, and the telephone 40%. The mailing is 100,000 pieces and you predict a 2.5% total response, or 2,500 leads. Using the 30% figure for mail response means you'll receive 750 leads by mail, 750 by fax, and 1,000 by telephone.

Now, when can you expect the response to come, over what period of time? Pierre Passavant has established what he calls a response lag time theory for direct mail. For a lead generation program as outlined in this example, here's what you might see in the weeks immediately following receipt of the mail by your audience:

Week	Response	Leads
#1	20%	150
#2	30%	225
#3	15%	112
#4	10%	75
#5	10%	75
#6, #7, and #8	5% (each)	113 (total)
Grand total		750

For telephone response, Eugene Kordahl built the telephone response lag time theory. Results of our example look like this:

Week	Telephone Response	Leads
#1	40%	400
#2	30%	300
#3	20%	200
#4, #5	5% (each)	100 (total)
Grand total		1,000

If this were your real, live program and not just a simple example, you might use these figures for planning. You would then carefully gather and evaluate what the true results were by both phone and mail by week. And assuming the quality was what you were seeking, you'd make adjustments and continue your direct response effort accordingly.

■ A "Live" Example ■

The place to start any program is with planning. It is basic; it is fundamental. But how and where do you start? It seems as if the answer ought to be start at the beginning.

Sounds simple enough, right? Yet, it hardly ever works that way. Because the question many times comes after the program has already begun. You started with some good ideas in your head (nothing on paper, or very little), a rough budget to work with, and an unrealistic timetable. Objectives—maybe, maybe not.

Not long ago I had an opportunity to work with a major bank on planning an extensive telemarketing program. Here's the background. The bank has been around since the end of the 19th century. It has over 100 branches and is "big" in its marketplace. It changed its name not long ago, updated its logo, hired some real marketing professionals, and is fast moving into the 21st century.

The branch system, however, is still operations oriented, not sales and marketing oriented. Some branch managers didn't understand at all and have moved out. The majority are excited about the new direction and need help.

The bank has a planned advertising program that is continuing and ongoing. Marketing wants to coattail that exposure and introduce some new products to customers. The idea is a direct mail program to a highly selected audience of current customers who are most likely to qualify for a specific new product. Followed with telephone calls from the branch where that customer banks.

On paper, it looks and sounds solid. Problems with personalization of the direct mail by each branch and other potential mail details can easily be controlled and solved. But what about the outbound telemarketing follow-up program? How is that to be put together? What is the plan?

On the pages that follow is the question sheet put together to gather the details of the facts, the situation, where and how the bank sees itself in relation to strategy and tactics, and a few thoughts about the methods needed to implement the program.

I share these with you because, as you carefully review these questions, you'll readily note The 8ight Point Market Action Plan is thoroughly covered. Plus, because this was the first project with this bank, some "get to know you" questions are included. Here goes:

I. What is the primary objective of the calls? The secondary objective? What do you want to accomplish—in the short term specifically, and in the long term?

  A. What is the design of the planned marketing program?

    1. What market(s) will be targeted?

    2. What product(s) will be sold?

    3. What volumes of calls do you anticipate per branch per program per person within each branch? Over what period of time? Will an inbound toll-free number be used?

    4. What advertising/promotional marketing materials support the telephone calls? How have you been servicing this marketplace up to now?

  B. How do you plan to measure the results of the program? How will you evaluate success?

  C. What is the bank's current marketing climate?

    1. What is your prime competition doing?

    2. What is the customers' knowledge of what the bank offers?

    3. What are your customers' attitudes toward the bank?

    D. Will the telemarketing program be a one-time event, or is the idea to make a commitment to continue calling on all or most projects?
       1. Will programs where telemarketing is used be branch driven?
       2. Will your branch people spend more, less, or about the same amount of time in the future making telephone calls? How much "dedication" to calling will these people have?

II. What job aids (sales support tools) will the people on the phones in the branches have to work with?
    A. Paper and computer-oriented tools:
       1. Will they access customer records via computer or from manual printouts? Are telephone numbers available?
       2. Will they have access to a single account record or to a complete customer information file?
       3. What product data are available for the product(s) they will sell? What form is it in?
       4. Are they trained to use the physical resource tools you have available?
       5. Will you also be calling noncustomers of the bank? If so, what information is available and in what format?
    B. What advertising and marketing promotional materials (fulfillment) are available? How will they be offered to your marketplace? By mail and/or toll-free number? At the branch? Other?
    C. What data will you want callers to collect on each targeted customer or prospect? How will they collect that data?
    D. How will the callers keep records of who on the target calling list has been reached? Who needs a callback? When? Who has been sent the fulfillment package and/or other information? Who has bought? Anything else?

E. For reporting, what would you like/what do you need in the content of reports? How often do you need/want to receive this data? Is there a system for you to get it as often as necessary?

III. What personnel will make the telemarketing calls?

   A. Who will make the calls from the branches?

      1. Are they in position at the branch now, or will they be brought in from other areas of the bank program by program?

      2. What job functions do they perform now?

      3. What is their level of experience with the bank? What is their level of knowledge of the bank?

      4. What portion of their time will be allocated to this calling program? Will it vary by project and need? Will the same people be used for each program?

      5. What is their knowledge and experience with the product(s) to be sold? How will product training be accomplished?

      6. What has been their experience working with customers? With noncustomers?

      7. At what level are their selling skills?

      8. At what level are their customer service skills?

      9. Generally, what formal training programs have they had in the recent past?

IV. What is the training program you will take to the branches on telemarketing?

   A. How much material do you usually provide in current training programs—manuals, tapes, workbook problems, tests, role playing? That is, what format are you comfortable with? How do you want this to fit in with what you are offering now?

   B. To whom should the telemarketing training material be directed? To management, those on the phones, or both?

    C. Who will give the program once it is developed—
your central training department, the branch
manager, or someone else?

    D. How long do you want the telemarketing program
to be—2 hours, half a day, all day, a combination?

    E. How are existing training programs followed up and
evaluated? How will this one on telemarketing be
evaluated?

V. What else do you think/know is important for us to know
that will help us work with you to get this program up
and running successfully and quickly?

VI. What is the company organization?

    A. How are the branches organized—what is the
reporting structure?

       1. Are there areas or regions?

       2. To whom do they report? How does this affect
the advertising/marketing/telemarketing
decisions to be made?

       3. How many branches do you have? Over what
geography?

    B. Is there anything else about the bank that may be
relevant or useful or nice to know?

Details, details, details! Yes, there are many, many specific questions, which the bank answered, one by one. The result was a well-thought-out plan that was developed and implemented.

It was very much a team effort. The marketing team from the bank and the marketing team from the telemarketing and training/consulting firm had lots of togetherness. And it worked, because the time was spent in the beginning getting the plan ready.

■ The Very End ■

This is what power direct marketing is really all about. After you've set your program objectives to be achieved within a set time frame for a set amount of money, clearly identified your audience, developed an offer, put together the creative, produced the program, and gone to the marketplace—you then analyze what happened.

What you may find interesting is that this *has been* power direct marketing in one form or another for most of the last quarter of the 20th century. Oh, sure, there have been countless technical changes, additions, and improvements. Still, the foundation, the fundamentals, the basic standards have evolved rather than changed.

So, "charge" is what direct marketing is about. It is what still makes power direct marketing "different" from other disciplines.

INDEX

ABOUT THE AUTHOR

Ray Jutkins is an international marketing and sales consultant and professional speaker. A principal of ROCKINGHAM*JUTKINS* marketing, Ray provides creative and consulting services to corporate and association clients around the globe. He is an active member of the Direct Marketing Association and National Speakers Association. He has authored over 300 articles on marketing, direct marketing, and sales in publications including *Direct Marketing, Target Marketing, Direct Marketing International,* and specialty newsletters. Ray presents keynote addresses and leads marketing seminars and workshops about 100 days a year. He has made more than 1,200 presentations in 44 countries on 6 continents. Ray lives with his wife, Nancy, on a ranch in southwest Arizona.

You can learn more about Ray by visiting his Web site at http://rayjutkins.com.

ROCKINGHAM*JUTKINS*marketing
Rockingham Ranch
Roll, Arizona 85347-7066 U.S.A.
Telephone: (520) 785-9400
E-mail: RayJutkins@aol.com
Web site: http://rayjutkins.com/
Facsimile: (520) 785-9356